THE
PEOPLE
OF
IRELAND

THE PEOPLE OF IRELAND

EDITED BY PATRICK LOUGHREY

APPLETREE
PRESS
BBC
Northern Ireland

First published and printed by
The Appletree Press Ltd
7 James Street South
Belfast BT2 8DL
1988

British Library Cataloguing in Publication Data
The People of Ireland.
    1. Ireland — Population — History
    I. Loughrey, Patrick
    304.6′094′5   HB3589.A3

    ISBN 0-86281-198

9 8 7 6 5 4 3 2 1

Contents

Foreword

A well-known Irish story tells of the death of a staunch Ulster loyalist. On arrival in heaven he was given a guided tour by St Peter. After surveying the celestial splendours he was surprised to discover a huge wall. It was twenty feet high and enclosed a considerable area. He asked St Peter what this compound was for. 'Oh, don't worry about that,' Peter explained, 'It's for the Catholics, they think they're the only ones here.'

Every Irish story has, of course, at least two versions. I recently heard this tale retold, but on that occasion those in the compound were Free Presbyterians. If Ireland, north or south, has anything in common with heaven it is that some groups prefer to believe they are the only ones worthy of being here.

This book is a history of Ireland told in terms of the successive waves of settlers who made Europe's most westerly island their home. The writers explore Irish ethnic roots and assess the importance of these various influences on Irish history and culture. Together, they convey something of the reality behind the stereotype – something of what it means to be Irish.

What it means to be Irish and who exactly can be counted among 'the people of Ireland' has long been a contentious issue. As two separate states emerged in Ireland at the beginning of this century their conflicting nationalisms demanded cultural and historical validation. In the south, a notional Gaelic racial monolith became central to the new nation state's image of itself, while in the north, preserving British identity seemed to demand the rejection of everything Irish. Alienation was the inevitable outcome for those on both sides of the border who did not conform to the pervading cultural ethos. Modern political polarisation was projected into the past to underpin ideologies which are exclusive and mutually intolerant. History was moulded to conform to the political status quo.

So exclusive does Irish nationality sometimes appear, that prefixes like Scots-Irish and Anglo-Irish are applied to indicate the degree of one's Irishness. A stereotype insidiously becomes the norm against which we judge ourselves. Labels like natives and settlers colour our perceptions. People whose families have lived in Ireland for hundreds of years can still be regarded, and can still regard themselves, as outsiders, as not really being Irish at all.

There has been much talk recently of 'the two traditions', of the planter and the Gael, to describe the Ulster, if not the entire Irish, dilemma. Widespread acceptance of this apparently diagnostic description indicates just how persuasive Ireland's conflicting nationalisms have been in fostering a view of society which sustains tribal preconceptions. Like all retrospective generalisations, 'the two traditions' is misleading; in this case dangerously so, for it contains within it what has recently been described as 'the myth of the whole Protestant community', and, of course, an equivalent myth of a whole, uniform, Catholic community. It does no justice to the inevitable pluralism that results from thousands of years of varied human settlement – to a complicated and contradictory story which fascinates students of history and which is outlined in this book.

Irish historiography has been revolutionised in the lifetime of one of the contributors to this volume, J. C. Beckett. Professor Beckett, with the late T. W. Moody, inspired and directed that revolution. Their rigorous standards of research and presentation at last brought more light than heat to the study of Irish history. Since then there has been a constant stream of research and interpretation which significantly advances understanding of the Irish past. For the general reader, however, the fruits of such research are often inaccessible. They deserve much wider currency in a country which cherishes its past and in which historical scores seem never to be settled.

BBC Northern Ireland offered an opportunity to reach a wider audience. We invited eleven of Ireland's leading historians to participate in a series of talks for broadcast on Radio Ulster and to our delight all eleven agreed to take part. In this book which is based on the series, Irish history is presented in terms of the groups of settlers who together make up the population of Ireland. We have aimed at neither a scholarly consensus nor a comprehensive account of all the groups who settled here. Rather, each writer makes a challenging case in assessing the historical significance of the people to whom most have devoted a lifetime's work. In so doing they offer a much wider than usual interpretation of 'the people of Ireland' – an interpretation which includes Irish men and women of every tradition.

As *The People of Ireland* testifies, there are no exclusive racial compounds in this small country, no high walls to keep different people apart. Rather, Irish personality and culture is an amalgam of the various influences described here, all of which must be taken into account by anyone who wants to understand the Irish past or present.

Patrick Loughrey
BBC, Belfast

Editor's acknowledgements

Victor Kelly deserves my first heart-felt thanks. He was consultant for the radio series and my constant confidant. His scholarship, good humour and good sense enlighten and inspire everyone who knows him.

My colleagues in the BBC were consistently supportive. James Hawthorne, Controller, Northern Ireland, was a gracious host and chairman during our recordings; he had complete confidence in this project from its inception and gave it his energetic support. Arwel Ellis Owen, Head of Programmes, his deputy Ian Kennedy, and Moore Sinnerton, Head of Schools Broadcasting, were also unstinting in their enthusiasm and in the help they provided.

I owe a great deal to those who gave advice and assistance as the venture evolved: Dr Brian Turner, David Hammond, Angela Fullen, Peter Logue, May McIlwain, Dr Brian Trainor, Don Anderson, Graham Mawhinney, Professor David Harkness and Dr Mary O'Dowd. I constantly sought the guidance of Douglas Carson, and am privileged to have him as a mentor and a friend.

Siobhán Kelly and Sanda McCullough tolerated the traumas as the project got off the ground in our little office, while Heather Macartney, with style and complete professionalism, saw it to fruition. John D. Murphy, Douglas Marshall and David Pritchard of Appletree Press have shown dedication to this publication well beyond the call of duty.

My wife Patricia tholes a lot; *The People of Ireland* project has been an all-consuming concern for me for the past two years yet she offered unfailing encouragement.

My greatest debt is, of course, to the eleven scholars whose work makes up this book. Despite oppressive work-loads they agreed to participate, they accepted the demands of broadcasting and met every deadline. Together, in my opinion, they have made a significant contribution to the study of Irish society and its history.

Picture acknowledgements

Page 16 (top) Ulster Folk and Transport Museum; 16 (bottom) Kenneth McNally; 19 (2) Office of Public Works, Dublin; 20-1 Kenneth McNally; 28, 30 National Museum of Ireland; 35 (2) Kenneth McNally; 50 (2) BBC Hulton Picture Library; 53 National Gallery of Ireland; 56, 59 BBC Hulton Picture Library; 65 Robert Vance Photography; 66, 67 Bord Failte; 68, 69, 70 National Museum of Ireland; 71 Light Fingers; 72-3 National Gallery of Ireland; 74, 75 National Library of Ireland; 76 National Gallery of Ireland; 77 Light Fingers; 78, 79 National Museum of Ireland; 80 Light Fingers; 82 (2), 83 *Irish Times*; 90 (top) Leiden, Bibliotheek der Rijksuniversiteit, ms BPL20, f.60^r; 90 (bottom), 96 (top) Office of Public Works, Dublin; 96 (bottom) *Irish Times*; 102 (2) Kenneth McNally and Ulster Television; 105 Aberdeen Art Gallery and Museums; 109 Eull Dunlop; 116 Light Fingers; 122 (2) Office of Public Works, Dublin; 129 National Gallery of Ireland; 130-1 with permission of the President of Ireland; 132 (bottom) Nick Scott; 133 Jill Uris; 134 National Library of Ireland; 135, 136, 137 National Gallery of Ireland; 138 (bottom) Bord Failte; 139 National Gallery of Ireland; 140 The Zankel-West Collection, United States; 141 (2) Light Fingers; 142-3 by kind permission of Oldham Art Gallery and by arrangement with the Electricity Supply Board, Dublin; 144 Light Fingers; 149 National Gallery of Ireland; 151 Linenhall Library, Belfast; 153 (3) National Gallery of Ireland; 157 (top) Deputy Keeper of Records, Public Record Office of Northern Ireland; 157 (bottom) National Library of Ireland; 162 (top) BBC Hulton Picture Library; 162 (bottom) reproduced with the permission of the Controller of Her Majesty's Stationery Office; 167 (top) Deputy Keeper of Records, Public Record Office of Northern Ireland, and Mr H.D.H. Cooper (Cooper Collection); 167 (bottom) National Library of Ireland; 170 Pacemaker Press International Ltd; 174 *Irish Times*; 176, 177 Ulster Museum; 183 *Belfast Telegraph*; 188 (top) Ulster Museum; 188 (bottom) National Library of Ireland; 197 *Irish Times*.

1

Prehistoric Settlers

Despite its rich archaeological heritage, Ireland has by world standards only recently been inhabited by man: its earliest settlers have, however, influenced the present landscape and created a significant part of the basis for the present population.

Peter Woodman

T HE prehistory of Ireland is paradoxical in that Ireland, after Iceland, may have been the last part of Europe to be occupied by man, probably less than 10,000 years ago, and yet it still has one of the richest archaeological heritages in western Europe. This heritage is so rich that we can easily become ensnared in the details of how tombs were built or the changes in the shape of pottery and metal axes to the extent of losing sight of the main aims of our study, one of which should be the question – how do we relate these relics of an apparently dim and distant past to ourselves?

If we return to our first observation – by world standards Ireland has only recently been colonised – it is startling to realise that human communities lived in Africa for over two million years, arrived in Europe at least 700,000 years ago and probably colonised southern England by 400,000 years ago. In other words, Ireland's record of human activity is one fortieth of that in southern England. What are the reasons for this difference? There is an undoubted correlation between the multiple glaciations of the more northerly parts of Europe and the apparent lack of early human settlement. These glaciations, which have happened on numerous occasions within the last 700,000 years, have, at times, created huge ice sheets which have time and again forced man back into southern Europe and, more importantly, changed the whole nature of the landscapes which they covered. In Ireland, for example, they removed most of a several hundred feet thick

layer of chalk that had covered much of the island. Effectively, every ice sheet wiped the slate clean with only 'flukes' preserving evidence of what had gone before.

Archaeologists refer to this period as the Palaeolithic or the Old Stone Age when, before the end of the ice age roughly 10,000 years ago, man lived as a hunter and gatherer with no knowledge of metal. If it had not been for these destructive ice sheets, could these Palaeolithic hunters not have lived in Ireland? It is interesting to know that even during the last cold stage which began at least 70,000 years ago, animals such as mammoth, hyaena and reindeer roamed the cold tundra steppes in Ireland before ice sheets eventually accumulated over most of the island. As we know that from 60,000 to 20,000 years ago human communities were living in south-west England, we must ask if these same people could not have crossed the sea to Ireland; in future years, we may be able to extend the antiquity of man in Ireland. Therefore, the second reason for Ireland's short history of human activity could simply be that we have not looked hard enough.

About 10,000 years ago, after several false starts, the earth's climate warmed up and today we 'confidently' talk of this episode as the beginning of the Post-glacial. Archaeologists refer to the hunters who lived in Europe at this time as belonging to the Mesolithic period and it is shortly after its beginning that the earliest evidence of man is found in Ireland.

Perhaps the best evidence for the earliest settlers comes from Mount Sandel, Co. Derry, where a Mesolithic encampment was excavated during the 1970s. This site, which lay in fields adjacent to the River Bann just south of the town of Coleraine, has helped revolutionise our understanding of the first post-glacial settlers.

The site itself, unfortunately, did not have the advantage of some Scandinavian sites which lie in waterlogged non-acidic deposits, therefore much of the equipment used by Ireland's first inhabitants has disappeared. This campsite lay at the base of the plough soil in an area of acidic subsoils so that little beyond the stone tools, the foundations of the huts and some burnt bones have survived. The most characteristic of the stone tools were deliberately shaped little pieces of flint which were used as barbs, arrow tips and knife edges. They are called microliths.

It would appear that these Mesolithic peoples visited the Mount Sandel area fairly frequently and built a number of huts in roughly the one place. These were about 6m across, presumably made with fairly large saplings, some of which would have been placed in holes 50cm deep. They were roughly circular, would have been covered by hides, reeds and possibly earth and had a little hearth up to lm across, usually set slightly forward towards the entrance. Outside the huts were large pits, possibly for storage, and areas where stone tools were manufactured as well as traces of other activities. While it was something of a surprise to discover the robustness and substantial size of these dwellings, other discoveries were much more important.

To appreciate the significance of these discoveries, we should first note that Ireland may have been an island since before the beginning of the Post-glacial. Therefore, many of the plants and animals living in Europe at that time did not find their way to Ireland. Animals such as wild cattle and fallow deer never lived there and many of the fish in Irish rivers are recent introductions, therefore one of the major problems of the island is to establish what was there when man arrived, i.e. what could he have hunted and caught?

Fortunately, at Mount Sandel, a considerable quantity of the food was thrown onto fires and was burnt. By being turned into inorganic debris, it has survived. From these burnt fragments, we know that these people hunted wild boar, trapped hare and kept dogs as well as relying extensively on fishing, in particular fishing for salmon and eels. So far, however, no early site in Ireland has produced evidence that they hunted red deer. Their diet could, of course, have been supplemented by plant foods such as apples or hazel nuts, whose burnt remains also turned up on the site.

We must imagine these earliest settlers living an organised, planned, perhaps near sedentary existence, probably in very small bands in an environment which would differ subtly from today's.

Of course, the fact that Ireland was an island coupled with the distinctiveness of its fauna raises the question of where these peoples came from. Ironically, the fact that much of the Mount Sandel settlement has produced radio-carbon dates of 7,000-6,600 BC reduced the probability of a convenient intrusion from adjacent parts of Scotland. In fact, the suggestion that the earliest inhabitants came to Co. Antrim attracted by the possibility of finding flint for making stone tools was an explanation of convenience which contained spurious reasoning. Nothing as early as Mount

Sandel has been found in Scotland and, until recently, nothing resembling the types of microliths found at Mount Sandel had been found at a remotely similar date. On the other hand, relatively similar industries were known from further south in Britain. Therefore, the idea that man first entered Ireland in the north-east and only gradually trickled out through the rest of the island is based more on the activity of archaeologists than on that of Mesolithic communities.

This picture has been altered slightly in the last few years. Firstly, Mount Sandel type industries have now been found in Scotland as far north as the Isle of Rhum. These could date as far back as 6,500 BC. Within Ireland, Michael Ryan of the National Museum has found what could be a summer hunting camp on the shores of Lough Boora in Co. Offaly, where some Mount Sandel type microliths have turned up. A similar range of little microliths has now been found at several sites along the Blackwater River in Co. Cork. Thus, wherever the earliest settlers came from, we can no longer presume that they initially landed in the north-east and we now know that, irrespective of where they landed, they spread very rapidly over the whole island.

In one sense, if man could get to Australia by 40,000 years ago, getting to Ireland after the Ice Age was not a significant achievement; however, the fact that an initial small population managed to survive in a diferent environment with a reduced range of resources was a real achievement. The chances of survival of a small population with biological and social factors also stacked against them are not great yet we can presume that this initial small group not only managed to survive but over the next two thousand years may have multiplied to several thousand and learnt to exploit all of the island's material and biological resources. At about 6,000 BC or earlier there is a sudden disappearance of Europe's standard microliths. Instead, a more distinctive local stone industry appears. This was based on the production of large blades, many of which were used without even trimming them into the variety of shapes so beloved of archaeologists. This can either be regarded as evidence of so-called cultural impoverishment, which is often supposed to hit island cultures, or it could be regarded as a sign of confidence in the settlers' ability to live with minimal contact with the outside world.

We can presume that by the beginning of the fourth millennium several thousand people were living in Ireland. Tasmania – a similar sized island – had a population of over 3,000 at the time of European contact.

While man had been struggling to colonise Ireland, other more long-term changes were happening in the Near East, notably the development of agriculture. At the very latest, this was brought to Ireland by 4,000 BC. It is usually referred to as the New Stone Age or Neolithic. Of course, actual evidence of farming is hard to find and instead archaeologists usually recognise the 'Neolithic' as groupings of certain types of artefacts. These include pottery, which is not found in this part of western Europe prior to the spread of farming. Of course, pottery rarely survives intact and it is usually the stone tools which show where the settlements lay. The most obvious new stone artefact is the leaf-shaped arrowhead which was made by using pressure to remove thin slivers of flint. The end result is a pointed arrowhead, usually 3cm or less in length and under 5mm thick. Although small, these would have been fired from bows as powerful as the long bows of medieval England – bows that could fire an arrow straight through a man. The rest of the package consisted of new types of scrapers and knives which, although less destructive, were not usually found on Mesolithic sites. The change is so abrupt that it could be argued that it was produced by the arrival of a new group of people.

We have to imagine the early farming communities of Ireland clearing areas of a dense oak and elm forest in order to plant crops and let their animals graze. While setting fire to the forest will achieve this to a certain extent, there is no substitute for cutting down trees – not to make ploughing easier but to allow sunlight in to help the crops grow. In these forest clearances houses would be built, the first proper farmhouses to be found in Ireland. The most substantial is that found at Ballyglass in Co. Mayo where, below a megalithic tomb, a house over 13m long was uncovered. This house was so substantial that some of the posts were set in holes 70cm deep; the framework of the house must have been carried on posts the thickness of telegraph poles. At Ballynagilly in Co. Tyrone, the walls of another house were made of split oak planks. It is sobering to realise that most of Ireland's Stone Age farmers lived in dwellings which were better than those in which much of the country's eighteenth and early nineteenth-century population had to live.

The Irish past and present are endlessly intertwined. This dolmen at
Glenmalinmore, Co. Donegal *(top)* was converted into a henhouse, while
during the Famine local tradition has it that a family of farm labourers lived
under the capstone *(above)* at Haroldstown, Co. Carlow.

Perhaps the most obvious sign of a change was the appearance of large burial monuments, usually referred to as megalithic tombs. The name ultimately derived from the tendency to use large slabs of rock (Mega-Lithos) to build the chambers and kerbs of these monuments. Even today, well over 1,000 megalithic tombs of differing types survive on the Irish landscape. These range from the rectilinear court tombs usually defined by a court area at one end, through the circular passage tombs to the small portal tombs (often called dolmens) and finally to the rather enigmatic wedge tombs.

Probably no other country in Europe is so well endowed with megalithic tombs. Many are scattered over the landscape in such a fashion that they could be seen as more than places where the dead were simply disposed of. They may have been important monuments for the living, giving communities of scattered farmers a focal point. In fact, while many of these tombs have contained a number of bodies, many of the dead may have been disposed of elsewhere. We know from Britain, for example, that in certain areas the dead could be left exposed in some of the hill-top enclosures called causewayed camps. One British archaeologist reckons that we would have the remains of over 600 bodies if he had excavated the whole of one enclosure in Dorset. Therefore, tombs like Ireland's northern court tombs or portal tombs, sites such as Audleystown court tomb or Slidderyford dolmen, may be the expression of something more than a ritual associated with the dead. In fact in some cases, the burial ritual may have included rites which ended with only part of the body being placed in the tomb – possibly, in certain instances, only the vital organs.

In this light, it is interesting to note that, at Donegore Hill, Co. Antrim, J. P. Mallory of Queen's University, Belfast, has recently been excavating the first certain Neolithic causewayed enclosure to be found in Ireland. Unfortunately, it is an area of acid rocks, so no traces of bones have been recovered. Is this an exposure site for the dead or is it a defended enclosure to protect families from the land-hungry depredations of their neighbours? Some British examples have been found covered in leaf-shaped arrowheads obviously fired in volleys by attackers. We know that these large enclosures were being built within the first half of the Neolithic so is it not possible, with a more settled lifestyle and possibly even an increase in fertility, that there was a very rapid expansion in farming in Ireland within a few hundred years of its arrival.

Of course, we are still inclined to think of these first farmers as a combination of American pioneer farmers living in log cabins and Amerindian tribes such as the Iroquois or Hurons. This may even be true for some of the initial pioneering settlements but this part of Ireland's prehistory lasted nearly two thousand years and in that period some remarkable changes took place, changes which probably do more than any others to create the Ireland which enters history several thousand years later.

Towards the end of the Neolithic, we can see evidence of just how large a population was living in Ireland. One of the most spectacular types of tomb to be found in Ireland is the passage tomb. These roughly circular monuments vary in size from 10 to 100m across and in this case the burial chamber deep inside the mound or cairn is entered through a passage. For example, some time before 3,000 BC, large mounds began to be built in the Boyne Valley. These were to form the core of the Bend of the Boyne cemetery where within sight of each other three large mounds, each around 100m across, were erected. In the case of Knowth, there was a mound 100m across, containing two tombs, each with its own passage over 30m long. In one, the cross-shaped complex of burial chambers has a ceiling well over 5m above the floor. Surrounding this large mound were *at least* eighteen other smaller tombs. Other subsidiary tombs have also been found adjacent to the other major tombs.

There is, of course, in the Boyne Valley and adjacent areas an extra element – art. Here in the Stone Age, geometric motifs – spirals, lozenges, zig-zags, sun bursts – were cut into the rock. Working with stone on stone is a long, painfully slow process. Yet some slabs, such as the entrance stone at Newgrange which is over 3m long, are masterpieces of composition in their own right as well as being the accumulation of hundreds of hours of work. One enigma is that, in some cases, these slabs were used in such a way that all or part of the art was obscured to human view. Obviously these tombs were associated with cults which we cannot even begin to understand. They are unfortunately unin-terpretable and part of a complex ritual which may include obser-vations of astronomical events. At Knowth there are paved areas perhaps associated with fertility cults while at Newgrange the mid-winter sun at dawn penetrates the very back of the chamber by shining through a little box perched on top of the entrance. The same general type of solar phenomenon can be seen in other tombs.

The passage graves of the Boyne Valley are Ireland's most spectacular tombs. Stone Age art at Newgrange is uninterpretable, but may well have been inspired by astronomical observations. *Overleaf:* Drombeg, Co. Cork, one of the best-preserved of Irish stone circles.

Place these tombs on little ridges in the floor of the Boyne Valley and surround them, not with trees, but with an open green countryside and we begin to realise just how much these farmers have changed the landscape. Yet this may nothing in comparison to the evidence now emerging from under the bogs in north Co. Mayo. Here Seamus Caulfield has uncovered large field systems which underlie peat bogs which began to develop by the end of the Stone Age. At Behy, Caulfield has found an organised series of field systems which runs for several kilometres in all directions. These are organised as a series of parallel strips running away from the coastal cliffs. Each strip is made up of fields of up to three hectares in size, and within each strip is a little enclosure which may have contained a dwelling. While we can never be certain why these field systems were created – perhaps through family ownership, or simply communal land management – they show that a certain pressure must have been developing on the use of land.

Caulfield has suggested that the special climate of the west could have allowed cattle to be grazed there virtually all year round. This might seem like a special situation, but Neolithic field walls have now been found in other parts of the island, including Kerry, so we must ask how much of the forested landscape had these farmers altered? Could Ireland's populations by 2,500 BC have reached 50-100,000?

There is no doubt that Ireland's Neolithic, with its monuments and field walls, was a surprising period, but the richness of the island's prehistoric culture continues on into the Bronze Age. Initially this period seems to lack the wealth of the archaeology of the Stone Age but a closer look would suggest otherwise. It used to be thought that metalworking was brought to Ireland by the same people who brought Beaker pottery about 2,500 BC. However, there is no real need to imagine waves of beaker-bearing invaders to account for a relatively minor change. These new ideas have to be seen simply as additions to an already existing society.

For most of the Bronze Age, metal tools either replaced stone forms or existed side by side with them. In fact, in the first few hundred years, axes, daggers and halberds were virtually the only metal tools. Not a major change, yet the products of Irish mines and workshops were exported throughout the British Isles and beyond – Irish artefacts have been found in Scandinavia, France and even as far away as Poland.

Besides some stone circles and alignments, this period is not noted for its monuments. The dead were often buried in simple pits and stone boxes. Perhaps prestige had been shifted to possession of bronze and copper artefacts which were often not very functional. The potential wealth of the period is, of course, illustrated by the numerous gold objects from the beginnings of the Bronze Age, a sign, perhaps, of the exploitation of native gold – but how much more significant if that gold was imported.

As a result of these relatively minor changes at the beginning of the Bronze Age, Ireland seems to have developed an amazingly complex and rich society some time after 1,000 BC. This is reflected in technological advances, quantities of implements produced and the beginnings of a more organised society.

The initial impetus would seem to come with the arrival of cut-and-thrust swords with leaf-shaped blades. These are perhaps the first specifically made weapon to be found in Ireland but at a later date we find more complicated techniques of metalworking in use. Sheet metal is used to make large cauldrons. In some instances, handles were cast directly on the rim. While most shields were made from leather, occasional sheet bronze shields have been found. The example from Lough Gur is the finest in Ireland but it is too thin to be effective. It would seem that prestige and show were very important. This is illustrated by the numerous finds of trumpets. Four were found at Drumbest near Ballymoney in Co. Antrim, two end blow and two side blow trumpets. Although musically more limited, the side blow trumpets, often over 60cm long, are technically the high points of the Irish Bronze Age as they were cast in one piece.

Wealth in bronze production can be matched in gold. Many later Bronze Age gold objects weigh over half a kilo, indicating that thin sheets of gold were no longer used. Exotic items such as the Gleninsheen gorget weigh much more. This wealth is, of course, reflected in the size of the hoards of gold and bronze objects from this period. The great Clare hoard contained nearly three hundred gold objects. Irish objects are also found throughout the western periphery of Europe and it has been noted that some of the richest hoards lie around the Shannon Estuary where trade from Iberia might be centred.

The most startling evidence of trade at this period comes from Eamhain Macha in Co. Armagh. At this site, Late Bronze Age farmsteads were stratified under a large mound erected around

200 BC. A monkey, a barbary ape, was found associated with the latest of the farmsteads. This was a society which could import pets from Iberia to virtually the shores of Lough Neagh.

This society of high technology, wealth and organisation apparently disappeared by 500 BC. Iron, unfortunately, does not survive well and it may have been its appearance which once again changed the nature of the archaeological record and created one of the greatest mysteries in Irish archaeology. Where is Ireland's Iron Age? There are few traces of Iron Age warriors in Ireland; there are some distinctive art objects such as the Lisnacrogher scabbards and the Turoe Stone but are these all that remain of an invasion of Celtic speakers who left the Irish their language?

If anything, the apparent continuity of occupation on some sites combined with the richness of the preceding Late Bronze Age would suggest that large-scale invasion was unlikely. Perhaps the introduction of the new technology – iron, and in particular the greater convenience and ease of obtaining iron ores – was the main impetus for the spread of a new language. In spite of the paucity of evidence, we know that there was an Iron Age society. It has left huge linear earthworks such as the Dorsey in Co. Armagh and the Black Pig's Dyke. It shows a level of organisation and confidence of use of the land not seen before in Ireland. But, unlike the heroes of the Sagas, these Iron Age peoples remain in shadows. Bringing them into the light is one of the major challenges of Irish archaeology.

This difficult challenge brings us back to the question of how this distant past relates to today's Ireland. Two points I feel are worth noting. Firstly, we should not use the record of prehistory to justify our prejudices of today. Sometimes the distinctly northern distribution of court tombs or the positioning of the Black Pig's Dyke is used to imply that Ulster always was different. This is, of course, to a certain extent true but in south-west Ireland the recumbent stone circles, alignments and boulder dolmens have a very narrow distribution, mutually exclusive of areas which today are noted for hurling prowess. No-one has yet claimed that Christy Ring's division of Cork into hurling and non-hurling areas was pre-ordained from prehistory. These distributions simply indicate that the south-west was frequently different. One of the exciting things about Ireland is the distinctiveness of its many local environments.

This leads on to the second point. The gene pool of the Irish was probably set by the end of the Stone Age when there were very substantial numbers of people present and the landscape had already been frequently altered. The Irish are essentially Pre-Indo-European, they are not physically Celtic. No invasion since could have been sufficiently large to alter that fact completely. Celtic speakers, Vikings and Normans may have made small alterations but it was not until the Plantation period that this gene pool was to be added to significantly.

2

The Celts I

The Celts were well established in Ireland a century before Christ, and they dominated the island for nearly a thousand years, resisting challenges and absorbing influences from other cultures for many centuries more. To this day the core of Ireland's heritage remains unmistakably Celtic.

Tomás Ó Fiaich

> Long, long ago, beyond the misty space
> Of twice a thousand years
> In Erin old there dwelt a mighty race
> Taller than Roman spears.

THAT was Thomas D'Arcy McGee's introduction to his well-known poem on 'The Celts'. It paints an idealised picture of early Ireland and its people, no doubt, yet it is accurate enough in depicting the Celts as tall and warlike and in placing their arrival in Ireland more than two thousand years ago.

Who were these people and where did they come from? The term Celtic is primarily a linguistic one, denoting one group of Indo-European languages. But we can transfer the name to the people who spoke them. Already before 500 BC the Celts had emerged as a recognisable people in an area comprising Bavaria, Switzerland, Austria, Hungary and Bohemia. Archaeologists have found valuable remains of this early Celtic civilisation at Hallstatt in Upper Austria and of somewhat later Celtic culture at La Tene in Switzerland. They spread over much of France and part of northern Italy in the sixth century before Christ, invaded northern Spain in the fifth century, sacked Rome at the end of the fourth century and got a footing in Greece and Asia Minor in the third century. The Greeks called them *Keltoi* and the Romans *Galli*.

Before they were finally overthrown by the Romans, they had left their name on Gaul, on Galatia in Asia Minor and Galicia in Spain; individual Celtic tribes had given names to Belgium, Bohemia and Aquitaine, to Bologna and Treves, Paris, Arras and Rennes. The greatest of the Celtic Gods, Lugh, had been commemorated in the names of Lyon in France, Leon in Spain and Leyden in Holland, not to mention London and Louth. Many of the river names of Europe are Celtic – the Rhine itself and its tributaries from the east, the Main, the Lahn and the Ruhr, also the Isar and the Inn in Bavaria. So also are scores of place-names in Central Europe with the elements *bri* (a hill), *mag* (a plain), *dun* (a fort) and so on.

The Celts were not, of course, the first inhabitants of Ireland. At the end of the Ice Age, as the climate became warmer – say about 6,000 BC – early migrants probably crossed the narrow sea from Scotland to the Antrim coast and gradually moved further south. They lived a primitive existence by hunting in the forests and streams and lakes. Next came the first farmers who used stone implements for felling trees and preparing the soil for grain, kept large quantities of cattle, sheep and pigs, and raised huge stone monuments to their dead like the tombs in the Boyne Valley and on the Lough Crew hills. Perhaps by 2,000 BC a new group of settlers had arrived, metal-workers in search of gold and copper, who fashioned the artistic ornaments now in the National Museum in Dublin, the greatest collection of prehistoric gold objects in Western Europe.

These were the dominant people in Ireland in the late Bronze Age when the Celts arrived. The Celts had the great advantage, for conquest, of having weapons made of iron. They seem to have moved into Ireland in two waves, one directly from the continent, perhaps from northern Spain or western France, into the west of the country and the other through Britain (which they had already conquered) into north-east Ireland. They may have begun to arrive as early as 500 BC and they were well established a century before Christ. To go further and try to estimate in what numbers or years the Celts arrived would be mere guesswork.

With their arrival a new era had begun in Ireland. The Picts in the north and other pre-Celtic peoples were overthrown. No doubt they still formed a strong element in the population but they were assimilated in language and culture. With the Celts it was diffe-

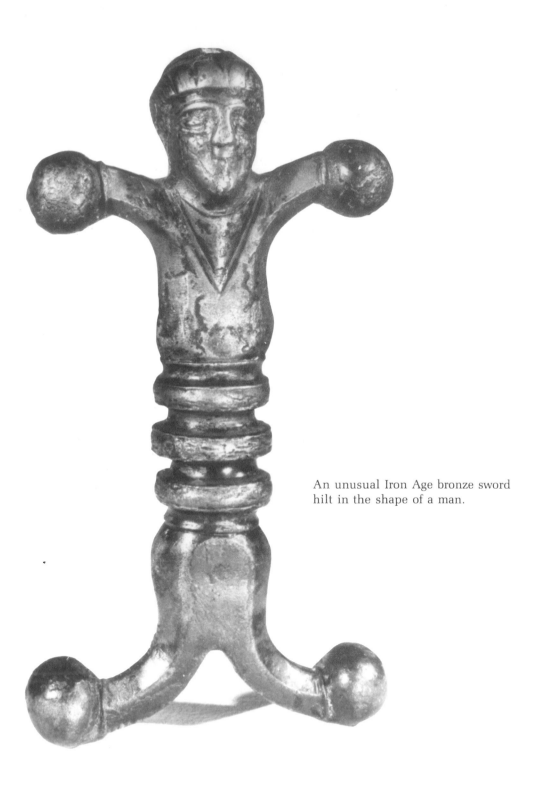

An unusual Iron Age bronze sword hilt in the shape of a man.

rent. They dominated Ireland for nearly a thousand years and even when challenged by other cultures they were to resist and absorb them for many centuries more.

Since writing arrived in Ireland only with the Roman alphabet, we know little about Celtic Ireland before the coming of Christianity. Roman writers called it both Scotia and Hibernia. But the epic tale of *Táin Bó Cuailnge* and other stories of the heroic age, written down centuries later, though not strictly history, are probably an accurate enough reflection of life in the immediate pre-Christian era.

They depict an Ireland divided into five major kingdoms with Connacht and Ulster at war, and the heroic Cú Chulainn defending the north against the forces of Queen Maeve. But the *Táin*, perhaps first written down in the monastery of Bangor, gives the victory to the north. In reality the Ulster capital at Eamhain Macha, the Navan Fort, near Armagh, was finally overthrown by the Connacht dynasty − perhaps as late as the middle of the fifth century AD − and the rule of the Ulaidh was confined to territory east of the Bann. From there they founded a colony in Argyll, whose rulers were one day to become kings of Scotland.

The most powerful king of the Connacht ruling family, Niall of the Nine Hostages, famous for his raids on Britain in the early fifth century, annexed the ancient ritual site of Tara and was progenitor of the greatest dynastic family in Irish history, the Uí Néill or the descendants of Niall. This must be carefully distinguished from the later surname O'Neill, for the Uí Néill were much wider, and included also ruling families which later took the surnames O'Donnell, O'Hagan, O'Kane, O'Donnelly, Quinn and so on. The descendants of Niall set up a new provincial kingdom in north-west Ulster, into which they later incorporated the central part of the province.

Each provincial kingdom comprised a large number of petty kingdoms or *tuatha*, so that the whole country had ultimately between a hundred and a hundred and fifty of them with a few thousand people in each. Local wars were frequent but not prolonged. The unity of the country was cultural, social and legal rather than political.

It was into this Ireland of warrior princes and cattle-raids that St Patrick brought the Christian faith in the mid-fifth century. I believe his choice of Armagh for his own special church can only

St Manchan's shrine, Boher, Co. Offaly, with its depiction of Irish 'wanderers for Christ' from the twelfth century.

be explained on the supposition that Eamhain Macha was still regarded as the capital of Ulster when he arrived. His missionary work was undoubtedly concentrated on the northern half of Ireland.

The Ireland where Patrick preached was thus a country with a long and venerable culture of its own. Like the wise foreign missionary of today he adopted a policy of what is now called 'inculturation'. The highly sophisticated designs which soon appear on the earliest stone crosses, manuscripts and metalwork were in the same tradition as those on the gold and bronze ornaments of pre-Christian Ireland.

Even the holy places and objects of pre-Christian Ireland – the sacred wells and stones and trees – were incorporated into the Christian tradition. The festival of Lugh at the end of July was baptised by the thousands who later honoured St Patrick on the Reek. The pagan festival at the beginning of spring was replaced by St Brigid's Feast on 1 February. Even the heroes of the earlier tales were given a place in the Christian pantheon. For example King Conor Mac Nessa was made a contemporary of Christ and died in an attempt to defend him, and Oisín was brought back from Tír na n-Óg to be baptised by Patrick.

The marriage of Christianity and Celtic culture produced in Ireland a society which was essentially conservative; hence some of its features remained unchanged until the overthrow of Gaelic Ireland in the early seventeenth century. It was basically a rural society with no cities or towns. While some of the more important monasteries like Clonmacnoise, Armagh, Clonard and Bangor grew into centres with a large population, one has to wait for the Vikings to see the rise of towns as commercial centres.

The ordinary homestead of the farming classes was the *ráth*, often erected on a hilltop and surrounded by a circular rampart and fence. These are the 'ring forts' of present-day Ireland. They have often left their imprint as *ráth* or *lios* on the local place-name, as in Rathfriland, Lismore, Lisdoonvarna, and so on. The king's residence was of course more elaborately built, as at Eamhain Macha, Clogher and Downpatrick.

Gaelic civilisation placed great emphasis on family relationships. The normal family group was the *derbhfhine* made up of all those who were descended from one great-grandfather. Each member of the king's *derbhfhine* was eligible to succeed to the throne. He was elected by the freemen of the *tuath* when the throne became vacant. The system had the advantage of ensuring that an imbecile or a cripple would scarcely ever become king, but it had the terrible disadvantage of provoking conflict between two or more equally qualified heirs. The ownership of land was also vested in the family group.

The king's inauguration was originally looked upon as his symbolic marriage with the sovereignty of his kingdom. It may have begun as a fertility rite. The feast held to celebrate the inauguration of a new king of Tara was therefore called the *Feis* of Tara, the word *feis* originally meaning 'to sleep with' someone.

The normal form of inauguration of a king was to hand him a white rod as a token of his sovereignty. Each kingdom had its own proper inauguration site. In the north the inauguration site of O'Neill was at Tullyhogue near Stewartstown. For centuries the inauguration flagstone built into a chair (*Leac na Rí*) stood on the side of this high hill until it was broken up by Mountjoy in the summer of 1602. O'Cahan, as the senior sub-chieftain, and O'Hagan, warden of Tullyhogue, cast a shoe over O'Neill's head.

The Gaelic king was ruler of his people in peace and military commander in war. He presided over the annual *Aonach*, which was often held at an earlier cemetery, and included the promulgation of laws and athletic competitions as well as buying and selling. The king of the *tuath* was bound by personal loyalty to a superior king who in turn was subject to a provincial king. The concept of a High King of all Ireland is absent from the early literature and only emerges gradually during the Viking period. Very few kings of the Uí Néill dynasty did not encounter opposition from either Leinster or Munster. The lower king showed his loyalty to his overlord by giving him hostages and accepting a stipend from him.

The learned class or *Aos Dána* formed a special group among the freemen. They included judges and lawyers, medical men, craftsmen and most important of all the *filí*. These were more than poets; they were regarded as seers and visionaries as well. After the conversion of Ireland to Christianity they inherited much of the prestige of the earlier druids. They wrote praise-poems for the king on appropriate occasions, preserved and updated his genealogy and were richly rewarded for their services. If the honorarium did not come up to expectations, they sometimes had recourse to satire, and were feared not only for their sharpness of tongue but for the magical powers which had been associated with the druids of old.

Like most positions in Gaelic Ireland the learned professions tended to become hereditary. In late medieval times the O'Davorens were the experts in law and the O'Hickeys and O'Sheils provided the medical men. The poetic families were particularly numerous: O'Dalys in many parts of the country, Mac a' Wards in Donegal, O'Husseys in Fermanagh, Mac Brodys in Clare, O'Higginses in Sligo, Mac Namees in Tyrone. Numerous also were the hereditary families of chroniclers and historians: O'Clerys in Donegal, O'Keenans in Fermanagh, Mac Egans in Tipperary, O'Mulchonrys in Roscommon, Mac Firbises in Sligo. The craftsmen have often ensured remembrance by engraving their name on their work: Noonan on the shrine of St Patrick's Bell, Ó Brolcháin on the stonework of Iona. Even in the church hereditary succession to benefices appeared as soon as they carried a worthwhile endowment.

The system of church government which Patrick introduced into Ireland was naturally the episcopal one with which he was acquainted in his native Britain and in Gaul. But he also rejoiced to see many of his new converts embrace the monastic life. Within a century of the saint's death new monasteries had ousted some of the earlier Patrician foundations and Ireland ultimately became unique in Western Europe in having its more important churches, even St Patrick's own see, ruled by abbots, many of whom were not bishops.

The early Irish church also developed its own form of tonsure in which the front of the head was shaven from ear to ear, and clung to an earlier method of fixing Easter long after this had been abandoned by Rome. These peculiarities gave rise to bitter controversy at home and in Britain, where the Synod of Whitby in 664 decided against the Irish. But no scholar nowadays, on the basis of these disputes, holds that the Irish church rejected Rome.

The sixth century is the great era of the new Irish monastic foundations. Many of the founders studied under St Finnian at Clonard. His twelve disciples were affectionately known as the Twelve Apostles of Ireland and each became an outstanding monastic pioneer in his own right; among them were Colm Cille in Durrow, Derry and Iona, Ciaran in Clonmacnoise, Canice in

Aghaboe, Mobhí in Glasnevin, Molaisse in Devenish, Brendan in Clonfert. Once the movement had taken off, it was imitated by others who had not been *alumni* of Clonard: Comgall in Bangor, Kevin in Glendalough, Jarlath in Tuam, Finbar in Cork. Religious establishments for women were far less numerous: Killeavy near Newry founded by Moninne, Killeady in Co. Limerick by Ita and St Brigid's double monastery for men and women at Kildare.

A sixth-century Irish monastery must not be pictured like one of the great medieval monasteries on the continent. It was much closer in appearance to the primitive settlements in the Nile Valley than to a fully developed Monte Cassino. A modern holiday camp like Butlin's would be closer to it in appearance than a modern Mount Melleray. But it was far from a holiday camp in spirit and the penances imposed for infringements of the rules had no equal in Western Europe.

The monks lived in small round cells constructed of wood or stone, like those which have survived on Skellig Rock, and the monastic enclosure also included a few communal buildings – the church, refectory, kitchen, library, scriptorium and work-shops. The daily life consisted of recitation of the divine office, long fasts and other acts of self-denial, study and work in the fields.

Scholars trained in the Irish monastic schools show an extensive knowledge of Latin classical authors like Virgil and Horace and some slight acquaintance with Greek. But their chief study was the Bible. Many of them reached a very high standard as copyists and in the Book of Durrow (from the second half of the seventh century) and the Book of Kells (from shortly after 800) they attained a standard of calligraphy and miniature painting which has never been surpassed. Indeed their artistic achievements in this field are among the greatest glories of Gaelic Ireland.

Colm Cille has been called 'The First Exile' in the well-known poem by Robert Farren, but he went no further abroad than to an area which had been partly colonised from Antrim a century earlier and where the Gaelic language had taken root. From Iona Aidan travelled to Lindisfarne in the next generation to become the Apostle of Northern England. The motive uppermost in the minds of the Irish *peregrini* was self-sacrifice – to renounce home and family and seek a secluded spot away from the world. Yet the names of these Irish 'wanderers for Christ' of the sixth to ninth

Life in an early Christian monastery consisted of recitation of the divine office, long fasts and other acts of self-denial, study and work in the fields. A twelfth-century monastic church at Kilmalkedar, Co. Kerry, preserves a rare sundial used by the monks to divide their day between matins, sext and compline.

centuries are still remembered with affection across the European mainland: Columbanus in France and Italy, where he died at Bobbio in 615; Gall in Switzerland, after whom a city, a canton and a diocese have been named; Fiacre and Fursey in France; Feuillen in Belgium; Killian in Germany; Donato and Cataldo in Italy; Fergil in Austria.

Not so well remembered are the ninth century scholars who flocked to the centres of learning in the new Empire of Charlemagne: Dungal the educationalist and Dicuil the geographer; Eriugena the philosopher and Sedulius the poet. We sometimes think that Ireland's links with the continent came to an end with the Viking invasions. In fact, the Viking danger was no sooner past than Irish kings and churchmen began again to travel to Europe on pilgrimage and built up a new series of Irish monasteries in Germany and Austria, some of which lasted until the sixteenth century. If the earlier monks had gone as far north as Iceland, these later ones went as far east as Kiev – no small achievement for men who travelled overland on foot and crossed the seas by currach.

If Iona was the first stage in that journey which led to Iceland and the Ukraine, it was also the first monastery to be plundered by the long ships of the Vikings in 795. The Vikings will be the subject of a later chapter in this book. Here I want to comment only on the Gaelic response to their arrival.

Irish churchmen gradually learned how to deal with the Norse invaders. Beside the church sites the round tower soon became a notable feature of the landscape – it was not only a bell-tower but a look-out and refuge for humans and valuables in time of attack. Stone churches built with mortar began to replace the earlier wooden structures. The greatest of the high crosses like Muiredach's at Monasterboice and the Cross of the Scriptures at Clonmacnoise made their appearence in the midst of the violence.

The Vikings were the first foreign invaders for nearly a thousand years and Gaelic Ireland found itself without any political superstructure for facing a common foe. When Brian Boru, from the obscure sept of Dal gCais in east Clare overthrew the Norse city of Limerick and later made himself king of Munster, he was technically a usurper. But the Uí Néill king of Tara felt unable to resist him and from 1002 on Brian was in effect king of Ireland, or, as he prefered to put it, *Imperator Scottorum* – Emperor of the

Irish. In a sense he was the first real *Ard-Rí*, the first who was strong enough to overthrow the Vikings.

Clontarf in 1014 was not a clear-cut engagement between Irish and Norse, but from then on the Vikings no longer presented a formidable challenge to Gaelic Ireland. Soon the Dublin Norse were largely Christian and sent their first bishops to Canterbury for consecration. But the reopening of links with Europe had convinced a new generation of Irish churchmen of the need to bring their ecclesiastical structures more fully into line with Rome and the continent. Because the twelfth-century Reform of the Irish Church took place in the same century as the Anglo-Norman invasion, we are sometimes inclined to forget that the reforming Synods of Cashel (1101), Rathbreasail (1111) and Kells (1152), the work of Celsus and Malachy, and the introduction of the Cistercians and Canons Regular all owed their success to Gaelic Ireland.

Like the Vikings, the Normans will also be dealt with in a separate chapter. Here it is sufficient to point out that even more than the Vikings they revealed the fatal Gaelic flaw of inability to unite. It was the interminable struggle for political supremacy between the provincial kings in the 1150s and 1160s that allowed Dermot Mac Murrough to make his appeal to King Henry II in the first place and induced the English king to encourage his subjects to go to Dermot's aid. De Lacy in Meath and de Courcy in east Ulster easily overcame all resistance there. In Connacht and Munster the young Norman barons proceeded to divide up Galway, Mayo and Kerry. So within a century of the invasion, the native Irish held only about a quarter of the land, mainly in central and west Ulster. Many of the new religious houses now excluded the natives, and a number of the bishoprics, including the primatial see of Armagh, were henceforth barred to them.

Yet from this limited base Gaelic Ireland fought back. A futile attempt to revive the high kingship was made in the 1250s, which led to the death of Brian O'Neill at the battle of Downpatrick in 1260. Perhaps its importance lay in the fact that Gaelic Ireland once more failed to unite around a single leader. Edward Bruce, brother of King Robert of Scotland, was no more successful at the battle of Faughart in 1318 and it was in the cultural rather than the political field that the great Irish revival of the fourteenth century was most effective. One wonders if any of the Normans really became 'more Irish than the Irish themselves'. In an effort to prevent further cultural assimilation the Statutes of Kilkenny sought to enforce a policy of apartheid on the Anglo-Irish from 1366 on.

But the Gaelic advance continued and by 1500 Gaelic lordships like those of O'Neill, O'Donnell, Maguire, McMahon and O'Reilly in Ulster, O'Byrne, O'More and O'Connor in Leinster, the various branches of the MacCarthys and O'Briens in Munster and the O'Connors in Connacht were semi-independent principalities – about sixty in all.

It was these chieftains and their followers, side by side with the two Fitzgerald houses, that put up the stiffest resistance to the Tudor conquest in the sixteenth century. First the Fitzgeralds of Leinster and then those of Munster were overthrown and by the end of the century Ulster was the only place left where the Old Irish were still in the ascendant.

In the final struggle against the Tudor monarchy Hugh O'Neill proved himself in many respects the greatest of all leaders of Gaelic Ireland. His vision of politics, at first confined to central Ulster, was soon broadened to include all Ireland and ultimately had a European dimension as well. An unusual combination of Gaelic chieftain and Renaissance prince, he recruited both Gael and Anglo-Irish in his service. The recently published book by Micheline Kerney Walsh, *Destruction by Peace*, shows him still unbowed after Kinsale and not the blind, drunken, melancholic exile in Rome whom some of his biographers have depicted. But when he went to his lonely grave in San Pietro in Montorio in July 1616 – now unfortunately lost – the poets recognised that much of Gaelic Ireland had been buried with him:

> There is a pall. . .
> Which quenches the glory of the Gaels of Ireland.

Yet the effects of a millenium and a half are not wiped out by a single battle or the overthrow of one leader. The Celts had left many indelible marks on Ireland and its people which have remained – thousands of habitation sites dotting the landscape, the bulk of the country's place-names and family names, the majority of its native saints and missionaries, its finest manuscripts, sculptures and metalwork, one of the earliest vernacular literatures in Europe, the majority language of the island until the

Famine and the only widely-spoken minority language today, a splendid native music, one of the richest folklores in the world. Later settlers added to them and adapted them, but the core remains unmistakably Celtic. They now provide a rich inheritance for the whole people of Ireland.

3

The Celts II

The once popular concept of an archetypal Celtic temperament – in effect an ethnic stereotype – has now been widely discredited; but while it is questionable if any group in Ireland can claim to be 'pure Celtic', it seems likely that there *are* some essentially Celtic traits evident in all sections of the Irish populace.

Gearoid Ó Tuathaigh

To many readers of this chapter it may seem a relatively straightforward matter identifying and assessing the specifically Celtic element in the history of modern Ireland, that is, in the Irish experience over the past four centuries. After all, when due account is taken of the abundant evidence of pre-Celtic settlement in Ireland, of the rich contributions of Vikings, Normans and English throughout the medieval centuries, indeed of the general patterns of cultural exchange which have been a feature of the Irish experience throughout history, historians have little difficulty or hesitation in talking about the institutions and ideas which characterised Gaelic/Celtic society in Ireland up to the sixteenth century. The ideas and institutions of Gaelic society, its social and political structures, its *Weltanschauung*, are all discussed overwhelmingly in terms of the Celtic continuum in Ireland.

Why, then, should there be any difficulty in pursuing and continuing to explore this distinctive Celtic element into the modern period? Can we not agree on a set of criteria for tracing the Gaelic or Celtic strain in the fabric of Irish society in the centuries since the sixteenth century? Can we not satisfy ourselves with a concise and coherent narrative of what happened to the rich and recognisable Gaelic society of the late medieval period in the centuries after, say, 1534? For example, should we not settle on the elemental fact of language as the key to the continuity of the Celtic consciousness, and simply follow the history and the fortunes (or, more frequently, the misfortunes) of Irish-speaking Ireland in the past four centuries? There would be nothing eccentric about going about our task in this way. For many theorists of Irish nationality the Irish language is the indisputable and unbroken link with the entire Celtic past in Ireland in the modern period; it is, in short, the *essence* of the Celtic presence in modern Ireland, as in earlier centuries. This, no doubt, was the point of view which prompted Douglas Hyde (scholar son-of-the-rectory and first President of Ireland) to hail the language revivalists of the Gaelic League as the only group in Ireland whose work sought 'to render the present a rational continuation of the past'.

There is, I would contend, a perfectly logical and intellectually respectable case for considering the Celtic consciousness or *mentalité* in recent Irish history as being essentially language-bound. Certainly a language-bound understanding of the Celtic continuum is less open to objection than many other criteria which have been used in defining and describing the 'Irish Celt', his culture, his temperament and his genius. The concept of race, in particular, is singularly inappropriate to a discussion of continuities in Celtic culture in recent centuries. Given the waves of migrations and invasions in the Irish past, and the incidence of intermarriage over the centuries, it would be pointless as well as perverse to search for purity of blood or pedigree in pursuit of the Celtic strain in the story of modern Ireland. The Celtic legacy is infinitely more complex and elusive than the mere counting of genes or the tracing of pedigree. So complex, indeed, that even the safe and sensible criterion of language is not sufficient to enable us to explore the full range of meanings which the word 'Celtic' has assumed in commentaries on Irish identity in recent centuries. Any attempt to explore even some of these meanings must begin with a reminder of the defeat and collapse of the Gaelic order in the great convulsions of sixteeth and seventeenth-century Ireland — *tonn-bhriseadh an tsean-gháthaibh* ('the shipwreck of the old order') as the poet Ó Bruadair described it. These were the centuries of conflict, conquest and colonisation, with a centralising monarchic state extending its authority throughout the island; the establishment of a state-supported church resulting in lasting and bitter community division on religious lines in Ireland; military conquest, the confiscation of land, rank and status on the basis of religious loyalty; the introduction of a new ruling class and a substantial (if unevenly-spread) community of new Protestant settlers; the inexorable drive towards the cultural (in particular, linguistic) hegemony of English culture over the other cultures within the islands of Britain and Ireland.

This process of conquest and colonisation was a protracted process; progress towards the 'conquest of Ireland' was neither even-paced nor without interruption. But by the time the process had been completed, at the end of the seventeenth century, the old Gaelic system was comprehensively defeated and, in a number of key areas, in the throes of rapid disintegration. As with all shipwrecks, there were some sizeable chunks of wreckage still afloat afterwards; these were to provide the rafts for some of the survivors of the old order for a considerable time to come. But Gaelic Ireland – as a vital political, legal and social system – collapsed with the military defeat of the Gaelic aristocracy which had given it authority and practical effect. As far as the Irish language was concerned, it is generally accepted that 'the demise of the native Irish-speaking aristocracy was to have a disastrous long-term effect on people's attitude towards the language.' English became the language of legal, political and administrative life, and overwhelmingly the language of economic and commercial life as well. It was the language of literacy, and in the course of time became the language of liturgy also. Marginalised from all the vital areas of public life, Irish became associated with defeat, poverty and ignorance. Those who were successful or who aspired to succeed under the new English order abandoned Irish and adopted the English language as quickly as the opportunity presented itself. The state system of elementary education from the 1830s, and the fact that English was the language of mass politics in the O'Connellite movements, further accelerated the advance of English even among the poorer peasantry.

The figures tell their own story. By 1801 a quarter of the population was monolingually Irish-speaking. By 1851 this had fallen to only five per cent, while less than a quarter of the population admitted to being able to speak the language at all. The heavy famine mortality among the poorer elements in Irish society drastically reduced the population of Irish-speakers, while large-scale emigration from Ireland from the second quarter of the nineteenth century largely to English-speaking countries strongly reinforced the desire to acquire English, and in effect, though not necessarily, to abandon Irish as obsolete and unprofitable in the modern world. By 1901 less than one per cent of the population were monolingual Irish-speakers, while the percentage who claimed to be able to speak the language had fallen to fourteen per cent. Moreover, by this time the areas where Irish was the normal community language were largely confined to enclaves on the western and southwestern seaboard, and even these were becoming increasingly penetrated by English. In short, by the end of the nineteenth century the language-bound culture which was the most unmistakably Celtic feature of Irish culture in general, was in full retreat towards the Atlantic seaboard. It seemed a 'residual culture', the survival of which was to be explained by the geographical remoteness and isolation of the communities who had retained it, a culture whose final disappearance could only be a matter of time and the final absorption of the peripheral, 'remote' areas of the west into the mainstream of economic and social life and into linguistic conformity with the rest of English-speaking Ireland.

However, as we mentioned at the outset, the linguistic dimension is only one aspect – albeit a crucial aspect – of the complex question of the Celtic element in modern Irish society. Indeed, in the conquest and colonisation of the sixteenth and seventeenth centuries the key determinant of loss and gain, of dispossession and preferment, of victory and defeat, was *religious* loyalty and affiliation rather than ethnic or racial criteria. And, contrary to what is widely believed, there was not an exact or total correspondence between religious choice and ethnic background. For example, with the defeat of the Gaelic political system, some of the Gaelic lords went into exile rather than accept a reduced role for themselves under the new English order; others of the old Gaelic aristocracy remained on, but generally under new and greatly diminished status, authority, or economic well-being. But a few of the old Gaelic stock succeeded in not only surviving the changeover to the new order, but in having themselves accepted and absorbed into the new ruling class – the new ascendancy – with remarkable skill and success. They did so by conforming to the reformed church, that is by becoming Protestants, thereby enabling themselves (if they played their cards right) to share in the privileged access to power and property determined by religious conformity and political chance. Thus, we find some Gaelic families (like some branches of the O'Briens of Thomond) conforming to the reformed religion, and over a period of time becoming overwhelmingly anglicised not only in speech but in manners, habits and general cultural identification. On the other hand, there were those of Norman or English stock – heavily concentrated in the towns and especially in Dublin and its hinterland – whose cultural modes were overwhelmingly anglicised, but who in the great religious cleavage of the Reformation and Counter-Reformation era remained Catholic. They suffered loss and discrimination because of this. They thus came to share in the common sense of grievance and of injustice which is such a strong mark of the Irish Catholic psyche from the seventeenth century. Indeed, it can be argued that because of the particular configuration of forces involved in the conflicts of the early modern period, religion was the key marker of community identity in Ireland from the seventeenth century. The interplay between religion and the more specifically ethnic aspects of cultural identity became extremely complex. The Catholic sense of collective identity – based on a shared historical fate, 'a shared sense of grievance, dispossession and defeat' – either subsumed or eclipsed other marks of cultural identity. A sense of Catholic identity did not necessarily (and increasingly did not in fact) mean a sense of Gaelic identity.

While the vast majority of the Gaelic-speaking Irish remained Catholic during the Reformation and its aftermath (with the majority of the Protestant communities in Ireland composed of those of planter stock, including, it is worth noting, Scottish planters of impeccably Celtic ancestry), continued adherence to Catholicism did not, as we have seen, require continued support of the Gaelic culture. For a time, it is true, the Catholic clergy were generally supportive of the preservation of the Irish language, seeing it as a kind of linguistic insulation against Protestantism. But in time this attitude changed. As it became clear that a mass conversion to Protestantism was unlikely, and as the Catholic bourgeoisie and comfortable farming class increasingly showed that anglicisation in speech and other ways did not mean abandonment of Catholicism, the Catholic Church changed from being, in the words of one historian, 'a negative collaborator' to an active agent in the process of linguistic and more general cultural change in Ireland. A Catholic revival did not mean a Gaelic revival. The so-called 'patriot [i.e. Jacobite] parliament' of 1689 did not seek to restore the Gaelic social or political order, but to restore property and a measure of power to Catholics who had lost both in the preceding century. The Catholic revival of the later eighteenth and early nineteenth century had no Gaelic trappings.

The new Catholic colleges and seminaries, established as Catholic self-confidence grew in step with the removal of discriminatory laws, saw English established as the language of Catholic higher education, and, as the priests went out from these seminaries in increasing numbers, of a more systematic and effective system of pastoral care and community leadership.

Nor was the cultural shift a matter of language-change only. The mission of a revitalised Catholic Church in the nineteenth century (and especially from mid-century) involved the systematic implementation of Tridentine practice in the devotional as well as the doctrinal aspects of Irish Catholicism. This occasionally meant official church disapproval and attempted reform or eradication of some traditional or customary devotional customs and social habits (e.g. in the waking of the dead) which had long been accepted as part of the Gaelic or Celtic cultural inheritance. Again, the social and moral emphases of the Catholic Church in Ireland in the mid-nineteenth century reflected or imitated some of the dominant values and virtues espoused by Victorian middle-class non-conformity in Britain (temperance, restraint, respectablity). In the drawing rooms of urban and rural Ireland the social standards to which the late Victorian Irish middle-classes aspired (and theirs was the dominant influence in determining cultural norms) were the standards which obtained among the British middle-classes. With the significant exception of religious belief and practice, by the later nineteenth century the more prosperous, or indeed even comfortable, elements throughout most of Ireland had achieved or accommodated to a substantial measure of 'anglicisation', or to put it another way, of incorporation into the cultural fabric of the larger (English-dominated) British society. As for those least affected by the process of 'anglicisation' – those whose speech and general cultural features remained substantially Gaelic – enlightened opinion assumed that this state of innocence was due to their remoteness from the main currents of modern life and that it would inevitably give way before the tide of progress and improvement which had already washed over the rest of the country.

Yet, remarkably (and in some ways, perhaps, paradoxically), it was during the nineteenth century – and in particular in the middle decades of that century – as the more 'objectively' distinctive aspects of the old Celtic culture seemed in rapid decline and doomed to extinction, that the concept of an archetypal Celtic temperament or genius, in effect an ethnic stereotype, was elaborated and came to enjoy a wide currency among the literate classes in Europe and especially in Britain. There were many sources for this sustained surge of interest in and theorising about the Celt and his distinct genius. Disciples of the Romanticism of the later eighteenth century settled on the Celt as a perfect illustration of the child of nature, wild, elemental, innocently alive to the promptings of the emotions and the senses. Cultural nationalism and antiquarianism both, in their different ways, sprang from the Romantic impulse. In Ireland, the flowering of interest in the Celtic past – myth, literature and legend, antiquities and music – whatever it owed to MacPherson's bogus Ossian, survived to sustain a succession of 'Celtic revivals' (Seamus Deane's phrase) from Brooke's and Bunting's work in the late eighteenth century, through Moore, and on to Ferguson (with his scholarly circle of friends and his excursions into heroic poetry); on further to Standish O'Grady, and climaxing in the most spectacular Celtic revival of all at the close of the last century, in which Yeats and Hyde (notwithstanding their differences in ideological and intellectual preoccupation) were the key figures.

External influences were crucial. The contribution of continental scholarship in philology stimulated a more informed discussion of the Celtic languages. The extraordinary spread of interest in ethnography – which, in a more sinister form, combined later in the century with versions of social Darwinism – was responsible for more ambivalent attitudes towards the Celts, ancient and modern. As with all major intellectual fashions, some voices and texts are especially important in the story of the nineteenth-century stereotype of the Celt. One such voice was Ernest Renan, himself a Breton, who registered what seemed to him as the inexorable decline of the Celtic languages (the distinctive Celtic voice) in the face of the new dominant zonal languages throughout the old Celtic lands (i.e. the French and English language). In his treatise of 1854, *La Poésie des Races Celtiques*, Renan sought to identify (and in large measure to defend and to celebrate) the salient features of the Celtic genius or character. Renan did not ignore the failings of the Celt, but the balance of his judgement lies heavily on the positive characteristics. Thus, for Renan, the Celt was possessed of an essentially feminine temperament – shy and gentle, giving full reign to the play of sentiment and the imagination, proud and loyal and with a strong sense of justice, deeply committed to personal loyalties and to the family, and this to such an excessive degree that it had 'stifled all attempts to attain more complex social and political organization'. This weakness in devising political structures had been fatal to the Celts and had resulted in their political defeat.

Here in Renan's profile of the Celt we have virtually all of the ingredients of the stereotype of the Celt which was to prove remarkably enduring. But it was not Renan (whose book was not translated into English until 1893), but Matthew Arnold whose version of the Celt exercised a dominant influence on readers in the English-speaking world since the middle of the last century. Arnold's Oxford lectures of 1865-6, published in book form soon afterwards under the title *On the Study of Celtic Literature*, were, on the face of it, a plea for the ending of the chronic ignorance of the Celtic languages and literatures in British universities in general, and in particular a plea for the establishment of a Chair of Celtic at Oxford. But Arnold had other and more significant ends in view. By using the Celt as a foil, Arnold made a sustained criticism of the materialistic and depressingly philistine character of the English middle-classes. As Seamus Deane has succinctly put it, '. . . everything the philistine middle-classes of England needed, the Celt could supply. The dreamy, imaginative Celt, unblessed by the Greek sense of form, at home in wild landscapes far from the metropolitan centres of modern social and political life, could cure anxious Europe of the woes inherent in Progress.' Arnold's essay was, above all else, the vehicle for a restatement – but with some important differences of emphasis – of Renan's classification of the essentially racial characteristics of the literatures of different people, and in particular the characteristics of Celtic literature. For Arnold there was a distinct and recognisable Celtic genius and temperament, and Arnold was as generous in his praise of its virtues as he was trenchant in describing its failings. Setting imagination, emotion and perception against a lack of balance, measure and patience, Arnold went on:

> An organisation quick to feel impressions, and feeling them very strongly; a lively personality therefore, keenly sensitive

to joy and to sorrow; this is the main point. If the downs of life too much outnumber the ups, this temperament, just because it is so quickly and nearly conscious of all impressions, may no doubt be seen shy and wounded; it may be seen in wistful regret, it may be seen in passionate, penetrating melancholy; but its essence is to aspire ardently after life, light and emotion, to be expansive, adventurous and gay. . . the Celt is often called sensual; but it is not so much the vulgar satisfactions of sense that attract him as emotion and excitement. . . .

Arnold's version of the Celt as the antithesis of the stolid, sober and (materially) successful but unimaginative Birmingham non-conformist was echoed in Ireland by, among others, Ferguson and, of course, Yeats. Indeed, when applied to the *real* Ireland of the later nineteenth century it is not difficult to understand why the unspoilt (preferably poor and uneducated) western peasantry came to be identified as the living repositories of the essential, the authentic Celtic *Weltanschauung* – in short, as the 'real' native Irish. But the Victorian passion for ethnography and racial classification produced a model of the Irish Celt a good deal more malign than Arnold's. This malign model, in which an aggressively Anglo-Saxonist ethnography combined with vulgar social Darwinism, classified the Irish Celt (by which was generally meant the poorer Catholic peasant) as being on a lower plane of civilisation to the Anglo-Saxon. This hostile view of the Celtic Irish stereotype is illustrated by Disraeli's denunciation of the agitating Irish in 1836:

> This wild, reckless, indolent, uncertain and superstitious race have no sympathy with the English character. . . . They hate our order, our civilisation, our enterprising industry, our sustained courage, our decorous liberty, our pure religion. . . . Their fair ideal of human felicity is an alternation of clannish broils and coarse idolatry. Their history describes an unbroken circle of bigotry and blood.

The special problems created and suffered by the enclaves of Irish immigrant poor in British industrial cities, the more violent assertions of Irish political nationalism (such as the Fenians), and the fact that Irish rural society (and landlord-tenant relations in particular) was deemed to be endemically violent, all combined to reinforce the more sinister and negative version of the Celtic stereotype — that of the dangerous, violent, unhygienic, simian-ised Paddy — in the main organs of British opinion especially in the period from around 1860 to the 1890s. The *Punch* cartoons are the most notorious examples of this negative stereotype. The stereotype was mobilised for ideological and political duty in countering a succession of Irish nationalist demands for some form of political autonomy. In particular, the stereotype was invoked during the first Home Rule crisis of the mid-1880s in order to provide an historico-racist argument for contesting the fitness of the Irish for even a limited measure of self-government.

A particular feature of the elaboration of the racial stereotype of the Irish Celt was the way in which, by intellectual sleight of hand, as it were, religious prejudices were conflated with the racial by publicists on every side of the debate. The Weberian version of the Protestant ethic combined with that of the dreamy but impractical Celt to explain why 'Catholic Ireland' did not 'industrialise' from the late eighteenth century and why the 'Protestant' north-east was the only area on the island to experience the Industrial Revolution. The legend of the defeated and dispossessed Celt meshed with the historical sense of injustice and dispossession of the Irish Catholic community. The term Celtic came to be used as synonymous with aggrieved or deprived Catholic. This, of course, ignored the actual Celtic ancestry of some of the industrious Calvinists of the north-east as well as the clearly non-Celtic cultural orientation of many Catholics, especially the successful and better-off Catholics. But in the sharp polarisation of communities in Ireland along a politico-religious axis in the generation before 1914 (i.e. Nationalist/Catholic, Unionist/Protestant) it became increasingly difficult for those who were unwilling to have their cultural identity defined or entirely subsumed in political or religious terms to find space or tolerance for the accommodation of a more complex version of Irish cultural development, in historical or contemporary terms.

There were, of course, significant exceptions. Douglas Hyde, while insisting on the preservation of the Irish language as the indispensable marker of a distinct Irish nationality, refused to accept that this version of cultural nationalism had any ineluctable political logic or religious affiliation. Indeed, in this regard Hyde belongs to a line of Protestant scholar-intellectuals whose interest in and support for different aspects of the Celtic heritage

A barbarous stereotype of the Irish Celt provided for the Victorian English a convenient justification for their political hegemony.

THE FENIAN GUY FAWKES.

DISENDOWMENT AND DISARMAMENT.

THE RIVALS.

YOUNG IRELAND IN BUSINESS FOR HIMSELF.

derived, in part at least, from their desire to find common ground between the different religious communities in Ireland in a shared sense of pride in and continuity with the Celtic past of their country.

But by the early twentieth century political polarisation had drastically reduced the room for making cultural choices of this kind. Political nationalism laid claim to the Celtic heritage, in effect the language, seeing it as the irrefutable evidence of the distinctive Irish nation for which a national state was being demanded. The more vague and imprecise (i.e. not language-bound) marks of the so-called Celtic temperament were likewise adopted by those whose sense of identity was primarily in terms of their Catholicism; it was an easy matter to translate the supposed spirituality of the ancient Celts into the fidelity and strong devotion of the majority of the Irish people to Catholicism, 'in spite of dungeon fire and sword'.

Unionists, (especially Ulster Unionists) opposed to the creation of an Irish national state, tended in the main to reject the Celtic dimension (in the past or in contemporary Ireland) as having anything to do with their heritage. This heritage was defined exclusively in terms of its Protestantism and its Britishness. After the political settlements of 1920-22 there were strong pressures at work in both parts of Ireland to establish an official version, as it were, of cultural homogeneity in each of the two political jurisdictions in Ireland. This had more to do with state ideology than with the richer and more complex cultural history of the communities in both parts of the island. In both jurisdictions cultural ambiguities and complexities of identity continued to intrude upon the certainties of official ideology. In the south, notwithstanding the formal state language policy of Gaelicisation, it soon became apparent (as any perceptive historian or half-genuine republican could have forecast) that Catholic and Gaelic were not synonymous. A substantially confessional Catholic state did not mean a Gaelic (or even Irish-speaking) community. In the north, not only was there an explicitly dissident cultural minority, but even for the dominant majority there was the dilemma that so far as 'Britishness' as a cultural identification was concerned assertion did not guarantee acceptance. Birmingham's image and understanding of Belfast need not necessarily correspond with Unionist/British Belfast's version of itself. Cultural identification

Douglas Hyde (1860-1949), by John Yeats. The Protestant scholar whose interest in the Celtic heritage developed from a desire to find common ground between the different religious communities in Ireland went on to become the first President of Ireland.

is not *only* a matter of choice; to be effective it also requires external validation.

A word, then, by way of conclusion. The creation of a stereotype – of whatever kind – is rarely a matter of pure invention. The act of creation involves selection and exaggeration, distortion and omission. So it is also with the stereotype of the Celt in modern Ireland. The quest for the Celtic element in modern Irish history and society is not a matter of genes but of genius. The characteristic Celtic modes (of thought and action, expression and behaviour) are not to be sought in the centuries since 1600 in distinctive political, economic, legal or, indeed, social structures, but in the structures of the mind. This structure of the mind – genius, mind-set, *mentalité*, call it what you will – is a notoriously difficult and elusive concept. It is, and has long been, a matter of selection, adoption and cultivation rather than of simple inheritance. Ethnicity, as Barth had pointed out, is not a 'given', immutable, inherited culture-kit, but a version of self which involves conscious selection, adoption and cultivation of key features, key markers of cultural identity. While it is true, as Estyn Evans demonstrated concisely and with commendable sensitivity, that the personality of Ireland has been shaped by the interplay over the centuries of the forces of habitat, heritage and history, the Irish have played their part in shaping that personality in recent times by self-conscious and deliberate cultivation and by their response to the images and opinions which others have of them. In sum, as we approach the end of the twentieth century it seems to me to be quite plausible to suggest that while it is questionable if any group in Ireland can claim to be 'pure Celtic' in any meaningful sense, it is probably the case that there are, to a greater or lesser extent, some archetypal Celtic traits or characteristics evident in all sections of the Irish population. This may be unsettling for those ethnic exclusivists in Ireland who demand that the essential or authentic marks of their identity be precise, tidy and verifiable. But to those with a more open sense of cultural relativism, and a more tolerant view of cultural variety, the suggestion that there is probably 'a bit of the Celt' in most of the Irish will cause neither surprise nor alarm.

4

The Vikings

The traditional perception of the Vikings as marauders and plunderers of Irish monasteries is incomplete: it concentrates on the early years of Viking activity, ignoring that the Vikings eventually settled peacefully, integrating into Irish society and making a positive contribution as traders and town-dwellers.

Marie Therese Flanagan

THE arrival of Viking sea raiders in Irish waters in the late eighth century heralded the first influx of new peoples into Ireland since the major settlement of the Celts had been completed in the last centuries BC. From about the second century BC until the late eighth century AD Ireland had enjoyed freedom from external attack or settlement. This was in marked contrast with the experience of neighbouring Britain or the continent during the same period. Britain, for example, like Ireland had been settled by Celts and at approximately the same time. But Britain, unlike Ireland, was also to experience conquest by the Romans in the first century AD and to be further colonised by Germanic peoples during the fifth and sixth centuries. By contrast, Ireland experienced neither Roman nor Germanic settlement. Rather, it was the Irish who engaged in colonising ventures between the fourth and sixth centuries, attacking and settling parts of Britain, notably in Scotland, Wales and Cornwall. This is an aspect of Irish colonial history which is generally overlooked.

In the late eighth century Ireland shared once again a common historical experience with Britain and the continent, namely attacks from Scandinavian sea pirates who came to be known as Vikings. The first recorded Viking attack on Ireland occurred in 795. In that year the annals of Ulster recorded 'the burning of Rechru by the heathens'. Although it is usual to identify the Irish

This nineteenth-century impression of a Viking chief reflects the image
of the Vikings as marauders and robbers prevalent at the time.

place-name of Rechru or Rechrainn with the island monastery of Lambay off the coast of Co. Dublin, this identification is not secure. It is possible that this entry may refer to an attack on Rathlin Island off the Antrim coast, that Rathlin was in fact the first place in Ireland to experience a Viking raid.

The term Viking conjures up for most Irish people bands of marauders and robbers who plundered Irish monasteries and churches, causing widespread destruction and terror, and carrying off the precious objects of the monasteries. Why did the Vikings concentrate their raids on Irish monasteries? One popular view is that the Vikings were pagans and as such violently anti-Christian. But the Vikings did not initiate raids on Irish monasteries. Less well known is the fact that the Irish had attacked monasteries even before the arrival of the Vikings. In order to explain why they did so it is necessary to highlight some less familiar aspects of the role of the monastery in early Irish society than the more well-known reputation for sanctity and scholarship which certain early Irish monasteries justifiably enjoy.

An early Irish monastery was often the most secure building in a locality. This meant that valuables, surplus food and sometimes even cattle were brought there in times of political unrest. A monastery might also be closely identified with its patrons and benefactors among the local lay aristocracy which had endowed it with its landed wealth. The office of abbot, for example, was frequently occupied by a member of the original founding family. The consequence was that a monastery could become a target for attacks during the petty feuds waged by rival aristocratic factions. The monastery or church of an enemy, since it was an integral part of his prestige, and probably also of his economy, became a legitimate target for attack in raid or war.

The notion that there was a golden age of Irish Christianity in the sixth and seventh centuries during which Christianity had made such a positive and beneficial impact on Irish society that there existed something approaching perfect harmony between the clerical and lay population is unreal; it derives in part from an unconscious projection upon social conduct of the high artistic achievements in metalwork and manuscripts of the seventh and eighth centuries. The reality is that early Irish monasteries were drawn into the orbit of lay politics. This is the chief reason why raids on monasteries had been carried out by the Irish even before the Vikings arrived in Irish waters.

It is nevertheless true that the frequency and scale of attacks on monasteries increased after the arrival of the Vikings. Whereas a monastery could have sought legal redress or compensation from an Irish attacker, it could not subject the Vikings to the same process of law. To that extent it may have suffered a greater degree of permanent damage.

What material gain did the Vikings seek from attacking an Irish monastery? A commonly held view is that their main objective was the removal of the precious objects of the monastery such as shrines, altar vessels and other valuable ornaments. This view is reinforced by the belief that the Vikings as pagans were bent on the deliberate desecration of Christian altars. The Vikings undoubtedly did remove precious metal objects from Irish monasteries, as is attested by their survival today in Scandinavian museums. The actual bullion content of most of these objects, however, is quite small, and they were probably valued then, as now, more for their craftsmanship than their precious metal content.

But the Vikings were also interested, and, indeed, probably more interested in the food provisions, the livestock and cattle and even the human population of monastic settlements, many of whom were carried off to be sold as slaves. The inhabitants of a monastery comprised not just the community of monks but also the tenants who farmed the monastic lands. The fact that in early Ireland the rite of sanctuary in churches and their surrounding enclosures extended to property as well as persons also dictated that early Irish monasteries were rich in material resources. In short, the economic wealth of eighth-century Ireland was most readily available in the monasteries and in a variety of forms.

All that was new about the Viking raids on Irish monasteries was the unforeseen source of the attack, namely from raiders who were pirates and who had travelled a considerable distance by sea. This was a potential source of danger which had not hitherto been contemplated by Irish monks. It accounts for their shocked reaction to the first Viking raids in Ireland as recorded in the monastic annals. The most enduring impression we get from the contemporary monastic annalists is the unexpectedness of, and unpreparedness for, attacks from seafaring robbers. In reality, plunder and robbery was a common feature of early medieval societies, including Irish society, and much more common than

Sirens lure a Viking ship in this illustration from a twelfth-century
Icelandic manuscript.

the outrage of the early Irish monk recording a recent Viking attack on his monastery might suggest. What was distinctive about Viking activity was that by the eighth century, Scandinavian society, as we know now chiefly from archaeological evidence, had developed highly sophisticated boatbuilding techniques and in particular a sturdy vessel with a shallow draught, a vessel which could be depended upon to undertake long sea journeys and yet was still suitable for beaching in shallow waters. It was this which enabled the Vikings to conduct the relatively common medieval pursuits of pillage and plunder further afield.

How should we assess the impact of Viking raids on Irish society and the church? Firstly, it is important to bear in mind just how long the so-called Viking period in Irish history lasted. The ninth and tenth centuries comprise a period of two hundred years during which Viking activity varied greatly in extent and intensity. If, for example, we averaged out the number of recorded raids in the period between 795 and 836, that is in the period before attempts at Scandinavian settlement in Ireland were made, bearing in mind, however, that we may not have a record of all the raids which did occur, it works out at about one raid every eighteen months. This would certainly not have increased noticeably the level of violence in Irish society. Between 795 and 820 for example – that is, a twenty-five-year period – the annals record twenty-six acts of violence committed by Viking raiding parties. This compares with eighty-seven acts of violence committed by the Irish themselves.

As for individual monasteries attacked, it is true that some of the smaller monasteries foundered during the Viking age, but the extent to which the Vikings were the major contributory factor has yet to be determined. It is certain that the major monasteries, such as Armagh or Clonmacnoise, managed to survive with their economic resources undiminished. It is possible that the demise of some of the smaller monastic foundations may have owed more to local political circumstances and the encroachment of the more powerful monastic houses, with their expanding network of paruchiae or filiations, than to Viking raiding parties. The monastery of Bangor, for example, was raided by the Vikings in 823 and 824. Bangor's location was certainly very exposed to Viking attack from the sea, but the weakness of the Dál nAraide dynasty, its political support, may have been a more important factor in its decline and apparent extinction than Viking raids. Only more detailed research into the history of individual monasteries will provide an accurate assessment of the Viking impact on the church.

Viking activity in Ireland entered a new and more intensive phase after 837 with greater inland penetration and the first attempts at the establishment of permanent Scandinavian bases in the country. By contrast with England, over half of which was under the control of Vikings by the end of the ninth century, permanent Viking settlement in Ireland was confined to coastal areas. How is this contrast to be explained? Nobody has yet suggested that the Irish were more effective militarily at repelling the Vikings than the English. Indeed there would be little evidence to support such a hypothesis.

One explanation offered by historians is that the Irish polity, the secular power structures, were so complex and fragmented, that there was such a multiplicity of petty kingdoms in Ireland in a continuous state of flux, that it proved difficult to effect a permanent conquest or colonisation of large areas of territory. It is possible, however, that it is not so much a contrast between the more fragmented polity of Ireland and the existence of larger and more consolidated political units in England, facilitating more extensive take-over, which accounts for the more restricted extent of territorial settlements in Ireland by comparison with the Scandinavian settlements in England or Francia during the same period.

The difference may be determined in part by factors independent of internal conditions in Ireland. For example, an important distinguishing factor between the predominantly Norwegian settlement in Ireland and the predominantly Danish settlements in England was that the Norwegians had a much longer sea journey to Ireland than the Danes had to make in the case of either England or Francia. It is also likely that attacks on England from Denmark were mounted by numerically larger raiding parties. Their leaders could retain a greater degree of cohesion among their followers during the relatively short sea crossings to England or Francia. That the fleets attacking England and Francia were in fact larger is suggested by the figures recorded in the contemporary sources for Viking fleets operating in Ireland and England.

Historians are increasingly coming to realise that it is necessary to look at Scandinavian activity in Ireland in a wider geographical context. It is noteworthy, for example, that raids on Ireland tend to slacken during periods of intense raiding in England or Francia, or during the Norwegian colonisation of the Faroes, Iceland and Greenland, and they tend to increase in Ireland when they slacken elsewhere.

What was the Irish reaction to Scandinavian attempts at colonisation in Ireland? There certainly was no united Irish military response. The individual Scandinavian footholds, such as that established at Dublin about 841, seem to have been absorbed rapidly into the existing complex Irish political pattern of shifting hostilities and alliances. The first recorded alliance between an Irish king and a Viking leader against a fellow Irish king occurred in 842. Thereafter, Scandinavian Irish alliances became commonplace. A simplistic notion of a united Irish army fighting to preserve the political independence of Ireland against an attempted Scandinavian take-over bears no relation to the much more complex reality. At no time during the Viking age was there a clearcut division between the Scandinavians as aggressors and the Irish as defenders. The battle of Clontarf, fought in 1014, has often been portrayed as a major victory by the Irish against the Vikings, as a battle at which the Irish king Brian Bóruma (Boru) allegedly defeated the Vikings and put an end to Scandinavian aspirations of conquering Ireland. This is quite simply untrue. Legends die hard and perhaps no legend will die harder than the legend of Brian Bóruma and the battle of Clontarf.

Popular conceptions of Viking activity in Ireland have been moulded by two different kinds of historical writing. The first, the monastic annals, emanated from ecclesiastical circles, and highlighted the plundering of monasteries. The second kind of Irish historical source dealing with the Vikings is royal propaganda tracts which were commissioned by a number of Irish royal dynasties in order to enhance their claims to kingship. The most important of these propaganda tracts is entitled the *War of the Irish against the Foreigners*. It was compiled in the twelfth century on behalf of the descendants of Brian Bóruma. It set out to depict Brian as the saviour of Ireland from the Vikings, detailing a series of ever more aggressive military campaigns mounted by him against the Vikings which culminated in a splendid victory at the battle of Clontarf. *The War of the Irish against the Foreigners* portrayed the Vikings as almost invincible, having no match in Ireland apart from Brian Bóruma, who ended a career spend fighting against them with a decisive victory at Clontarf which finally freed Ireland from the threat of a Scandinavian take-over. As the very title suggests, its intention was to imply a united Irish opposition to Scandinavian activity in Ireland. This pseudo-historical propaganda tract was written to enhance the prestige of the twelfth-century descendants of Brian Bóruma.

The reality is that the battle of Clontarf was occasioned by a revolt of the king of Leinster against the overlordship of Brian Bóruma. It was a battle of Munstermen against Leinstermen with Vikings participating on both sides, the Scandinavians of Limerick and Waterford fighting on behalf of Brian Bóruma and the Scandinavian king of Dublin fighting on behalf of the king of Leinster, to whom he was related by marriage.

Just as there never was a unity of purpose on the part of the Irish against the Vikings, so there never was a unity of purpose among the Scandinavians in Ireland. In the 850s, for example, Dane had fought Norwegian for control of the Scandinavian settlement at Dublin.

In the late ninth century Viking activity and interest in Ireland had slackened temporarily and almost ceased for approximately forty years. In 902 the Scandinavian settlement which had been established at Dublin was actually abandoned. But in the second decade of the tenth century, that is from about 920, a new Scandinavian movement into Ireland began again, at a time when the Vikings were finding that their activities were being curtailed in other parts of Europe. This phase of activity has been designated by some historians as the second Viking age. A similar sequence of events to that of the first Viking age occurred with an initial phase of raiding, followed by attempts at establishing permanent bases. These once again proved enduring only along the coast. A Scandinavian settlement at Dublin was re-established in 917. The Scandinavian settlements at Limerick, Waterford and Wexford also date from the so-called second Viking age.

By the mid-tenth century these Scandinavians had settled permanently and peacefully in Ireland. They had been absorbed and assimilated into Irish society. Although we know little about the process, they had converted to Christianity. The death, for example, of Olaf, king of Dublin, at the monastery of Iona after a 'victory of repentance' is recorded in 980. From the mid-tenth century historians are justified in speaking of the Hiberno-Norse rather than the Vikings of Ireland, such was the level of integration and inter-marriage into Irish society. If we take language as a yardstick of that integration, the old Norse language of the settlers did not survive beyond a selection of loan words which were borrowed into Irish mostly for terms which did not already exist in the Irish language. These loan words, which relate to fishing, shipping and trade, reflect the areas in which the Scandinavian settlers made a positive impact on Irish society.

The Scandinavians were to make their most enduring contribution to Ireland as traders and town dwellers. It is a commonplace to say that the Scandinavians founded the first towns in Ireland; in recent years historians have qualified this view in some respects. Some scholars now argue that certain Irish monasteries had such a large population and were organised both physically and economically in such a way as to constitute a native Irish form of urban settlement. Terms such as 'proto-town' or 'pre-urban nucleus' have become popular, both with professional archaeologists and historians, to describe the larger Irish monasteries. This is a useful insight and incidentally helps to elucidate further why both the Irish and the Scandinavians attacked monastic sites.

Nevertheless, it remains true that even if the larger Irish monasteries may be classed as native Irish towns the Scandinavians founded a different kind of urban settlement in Ireland, one which pursued manufacturing and trade not just for the Irish market but also engaged in overseas trade.

The importance of overseas trade is highlighted by the establishment of a mint at Dublin in 997. The coins produced at Dublin were exact copies of the contemporary English silver pennies and were obviously struck primarily for use in trade with England. For the first few decades of the tenth century Dublin had been just one of a number of growing Viking towns. If one of these towns stood out it was perhaps Limerick. However, Dublin's natural harbour, its eastward prospect and its potential for taking a share of long-distance trade along a route which linked the Scandinavian lands with western France and the Mediterranean via the Irish Sea, and for conducting business across the Irish Sea, were to make it in time Ireland's principal town.

An Iron Age idol, probably of the Celtic war god Nuada of the Silver Hand, from Armagh, one of the earliest representations of the human form in Ireland.

The crannog at Craggaunowen, Co. Clare, a reconstruction of a defensive lake dwelling, some of which were still in use as late as the seventeenth century.

Dún Óghil, an Iron Age fort on Inishmore in the Aran Islands. The more modern stone wall enclosures are reminiscent of field systems unearthed at Behy, Co. Mayo, which date from 3000 BC.

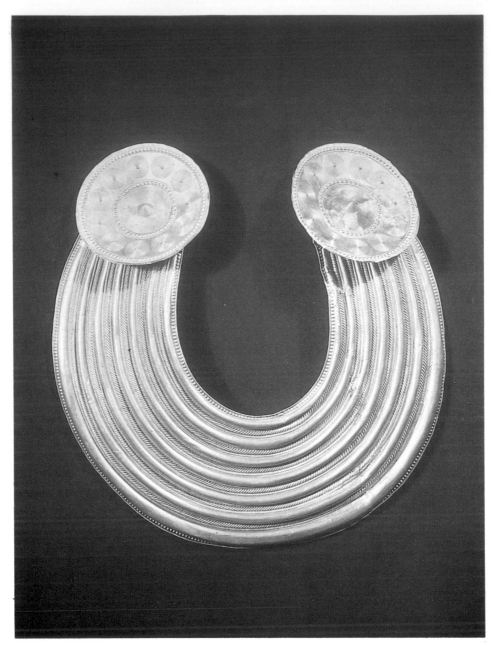

This gold collar was discovered in a rock fissure at Gleninsheen, Co. Clare, in 1932. The discovery and exploitation of native gold made Ireland a gold-working centre during the later Bronze Age.

The Domnach Airgid, a silver reliquary from the early Christian period. For centuries it was in the keeping of the Maguires, Gaelic chieftains of Co. Fermanagh.

Bronze crucifixion plaque from Clonmacnoise, Co. Offaly. The image of the crucified Christ became the most important of all Irish Christian symbols. *Opposite:* Ancient and modern High Crosses at Castledermot, Co. Kildare. Early Christian High Crosses were the model for many imitations during the Gaelic revival.

Overleaf: The Marriage of Strongbow and Aoife by Daniel Maclise. The arrival of the Normans marked the beginning of the end of the old Gaelic order. Maclise's huge canvas of the marriage of convenience made between the daughter of Dermot MacMurrough and the Norman earl mirrors the Romantic nationalist view of the conquest and colonisation of Ireland prevalent in the late nineteenth century.

Hibernian Man and Woman. Following the Romantic movement, the nineteenth century saw a succession of Celtic 'revivals' which presented an idealised racial stereotype of the Celt. The somewhat heroic figures above are from a series of aquatint drawings of historical British and Irish dress by an early nineteenth-century antiquarian, Charles H. Smith.

Opposite: Romantic speculation on the mysterious ancient Celts centred on the Druids. Smith's drawing made a tremendous impression on the popular image of the Celtic priesthood, and served as a model for the regalia and dress of modern Druids.

In the Victorian period the malign model of the Irishman as subhuman
savage found in the *Punch* cartoons of Tenniel and others was paralleled by
a romanticised view of the Celt as unspoilt and innocent peasant, as seen in
Augustus Burke's portrait, *A Connemara Girl.*
Opposite: Modern pilgrims on the holy mountain of Croagh Patrick continue
a religious tradition which dates back to the pre-Christian festival of
Lughnasa.

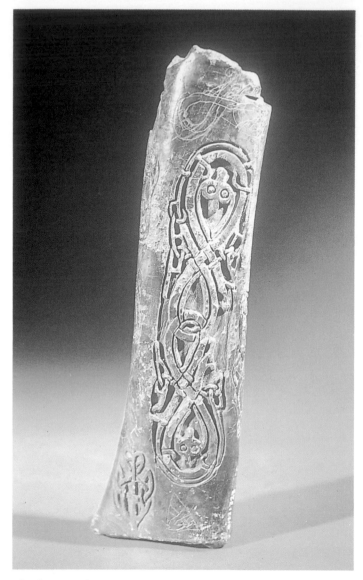

The fusion of Celtic and Viking styles created a hybrid of decoration seen in this bone trial piece found near Dungarvan, Co. Waterford.

Viking Ireland was part of a wide network of trade which stretched across northern Europe. This ivory chess piece of a queen (right) discovered in Co. Meath probably came from the same workshop in the Orkneys which produced the Lewis Chessmen now in the British Museum. Similar pieces have been found as far afield as Sweden and northern Italy.

The largest castle in Ireland and former stronghold of the Norman lordship of Meath, Trim Castle resembles dozens of contemporary fortresses in Britain and northern France.

The fact that Dublin became the capital of Ireland was determined by the economic importance of its mercantile connections in the tenth and eleventh centuries. Archaeological excavations in Dublin over the last two decades have revealed the extent of its activities as a manufacturing and trading centre. Dublin had specialised craftsmen, especially bronze-smiths, combmakers and leatherworkers. Imported items recovered also revealed the extent of Dublin's external trading contacts. Some time after the middle of the eleventh century the fine metalworkers of Dublin began producing goods for the Irish hinterland. By the end of the eleventh century Scandinavian styles and tastes were exercising a dominant influence on Irish artwork produced in such native centres as Clonmacnoise.

The small Hiberno-Norse colonies centred on the trading towns of Dublin, Waterford, Wexford, Limerick and Cork were not politically powerful. On the contrary, they were all subjected from the mid-tenth century to the overlordship of the more powerful of the Irish kings. But the Scandinavian towns did constitute an important dynamic element in Irish society, engaging in an expanding trade and increasingly influencing Ireland's communications with the outside world. They provided an important additional source of wealth for those Irish kings who subjected them to their overlordship, chiefly in the form of silver exacted as tribute or rents. The more powerful Irish kings also learned to use ships, at sea and on the rivers and lakes in their military manoeuvres.

The positive and enduring benefits accruing from the Hiberno-Norse settlements more than offset the short-term limited destructive effects of the period of Viking raids, which have been so highlighted in the past. The traditional perception of the Vikings as merely robbers and plunderers, as negative and destructive irritants of Irish society, was derived largely from the monastic annalists. It has been modified considerably by historical and archaeological research in recent years; in the case of Ireland, particularly by the archaeological evidence emanating from Dublin in the last two decades. The Dublin excavations attested to the peaceful and productive co-existence with an integration into Irish society of the Vikings.

The long-running controversy between developers and archaeologists which occurred at the site of the Wood Quay excavations in Dublin during the 1970s forced the citizens of Dublin

The site at Wood Quay, centre of
Viking Dublin.
Left: Archaeologists discover the
bones of a child on the last day of
the excavation.

'A convincing vote in favour of the Viking heritage': protest march against proposals to build high rise offices for Dublin Corporation on the Wood Quay site. The protests failed.

at least to re-evaluate the Viking contribution to their city. The result was a convincing vote in favour of the Viking heritage. On 23 September 1978 no less than 15,000 people marched to protest against proposals to build high-rise offices for Dublin Corporation on the Wood Quay site. And over a quarter of a million people signed a petition for its preservation. They lobbied to preserve the Viking contribution to the foundation of the city of Dublin, which they had come to perceive as valuable and important. Although offices for Dublin Corporation were subsequently built on the Wood Quay site, the enduring victory of the Wood Quay protest has been the enriched understanding and popular enthusiasm and concern for the Viking contribution to their origins among the present generation of Dubliners, a re-evaluation which hopefully will be absorbed by all the inhabitants of Ireland.

The preoccupation with Viking violence in the past obscured the process of settlement and integration of the Vikings into Irish society. Once the Viking settlers were converted to Christianity, once intermarriage took place and once local roots were put down, the Vikings made no effort or had no desire to stand apart from Irish society. The Viking age in Ireland ended with the Scandinavian settlers becoming part of Irish society.

5

The Normans

After a period of isolation Ireland was in the twelfth century drawn back into the mainstream of western history: the agents of this were the Normans, who were to have a profound effect on the social and economic life of the country and on the way it is governed.

Lewis Warren

I s Ireland a part of Europe? The answer to that question depends upon what period of history we are talking about. Sometimes it is and sometimes it is not. In the remote past Ireland had been a part of a far-flung Celtic society. But when the Roman empire spread out to embrace other Celtic lands into a civilisation based on the Mediterranean, Ireland was left out, cut off and detached. Later, after the Roman empire in the west had disintegrated, Ireland helped a struggling Europe to its feet, preaching the gospel to the barbarians and teaching them how to read and write. In the ninth century Irish scholars were prominent at the court of Emperor Charlemagne and his successors. But then, when Europe developed its own momentum of change and progress, Ireland retreated in upon itself, seeming to shun the world outside. In the twelfth century something unusual happened: Europe itself reached out to Ireland as if to draw it back into the mainstream of western history. The agents of it were men who spoke French. We usually call them the Normans. They reached Ireland via England and Wales.

Being taken over by the Normans is an experience which the Irish share with the English. The outcome of that experience was very different in each case. Why is an interesting question. The answer commonly given is that England was completely conquered by the Normans and Ireland was not; the implication being that this is why England emerged as a well-organised state with an effective central authority, and Ireland was left as a political mess. But this is a very superficial and inadequate answer. We do not yet have a better answer because until very recently historians have not been accustomed to comparing the history of one country with another. Part of the legacy of nineteenth-century nationalism has been the assumption that nations have unique histories. For far too long we have been accustomed to partition history into compartments, as the history of England, the history of Ireland, the history of Scotland, instead of the history of the British Isles. It is of course convenient to partition history into manageable portions; but all too often we forget to open the connecting doors between the compartments.

This has serious consequences. It shuts us off from instructive parallels, and makes our judgements about the past short-sighted and unbalanced. Let me give you a small but significant example: in 1217 the government in England issued an order to its governor in Ireland that he was not in future to allow any Irishman to be appointed to high ecclesiastical office, but was to secure the appointment of worthy Englishmen. This, of course, is seen as anti-Irish and racist, and as typical of the antagonism between incomers and natives which lies at the root of the 'Irish problem'. Recently, however, I came across an exact parallel in English history: William the Conqueror ordered that no Englishmen were to be appointed as bishops or abbots. I came across this by chance; I had never read of it in English history books. English historians take for granted that the Norman conquest involved Normanisation in church and state. The Normans were a few thousand in a population of two million. To survive and get a grip on the country they had to seize control of all positions of authority. William's order was not racist, it was hard political necessity, ruthless but understandable. It was totally effective; Englishmen were eliminated from the higher ranks of the church for nigh on a hundred years. By contrast that order to the governor of Ireland in 1217 had only marginal effect and was rescinded after ten years. The English suffered far more from the Normans than the Irish ever did. In Domesday Book there is no trace of the great families which had ruled England before 1066; in Ireland the leading families whose names are familiar from long before the Normans arrived are still there four hundred years later.

The Normans, of course, arrived a century later in Ireland than in England. Many historians have questioned whether we should speak of 'Normans' in Ireland. Only a very few of the earliest incomers had been born in Normandy or held estates there; admittedly they certainly took a pride in their Norman ancestry, but for most of them the family links were remote, and their interests were much more bound up with the kingdom of England. So many historians call them 'Anglo-Normans'. There is an important point here which I do not dispute, but which I will ignore for one overriding reason: being a Norman was not a matter of where you were born, it was a state of mind. It involved identifying with what was believed to be the distinctiveness of people of Norman stock which marked them out for a special destiny. Like all such beliefs it rested on myth-making; but it was nourished and fortified by the remarkable history of the Normans.

Normandy is that province of France along the Channel coast which was taken over in the tenth century by Vikings; Normandy is the land of the *nordmanni* – the northmen. The Normans regarded their Viking origins as setting them apart from their neighbours; but in fact is is very hard to trace Scandinavian influence in Normandy, so we have to assume that the Vikings were few in number and soon became Frenchified in language and customs. For a century or so Normandy was backward, illiterate, and ramshackle. Then quite remarkably in the eleventh century Normandy was transformed into a well-organised, powerful ministate. In the middle of the century it erupted, like a volcano sending out streams of lava. From 1066 the lava flowed over the Channel, engulfed the whole of England, flowed into Scotland over the Lowlands, right round the eastern seaboard and into Galloway, edged its way into the Welsh valleys and spread out over the lower lands of south Wales and then in 1169 spilled over into Ireland. And that is not all, for even before 1066 Normans had been flowing south to southern Italy.

There are different stories about the start of the southern saga. Norman historians liked to tell of a party of Normans returning from a pilgrimage to the Holy Land, landing at Salerno, finding it besieged by Moslems, coming to the rescue, and being invited to stay on. Italian historians tell of some Norman expelled from Normandy going to Rome to complain to the pope and being advised that there was a rebellion going on against Byzantine rule in southern Italy and their help would be very welcome. The papacy must soon have regretted encouraging the Normans to serve as mercenaries. Southern Italy was politically fragmented, and the Normans exploited every opportunity to set themselves up as robber barons. Pope Leo IX decided to get rid of them. He persuaded all the factions in Italy to join forces against them, and brought in from Germany a contingent of the emperor's finest troops. At Civitate in 1053 a hopelessly outnumbered band of Normans, bedraggled and hungry because their supplies had been cut off, took on the pope's army and routed it. They fell on their knees before the pope to beg his forgiveness and carried him off as their prisoner. Within twenty years they had taken control of all of Italy south of Rome. They crossed the straits of Messina and invaded Sicily, which was then under Arab rule. At the very same time as William the Conqueror was subduing England the Normans in the south were subduing Sicily. From there they menaced three empires: the Arabs in North Africa and the Middle East, the Byzantines in the Balkans, and the German emperors who controlled Lombardy and aspired to take over all of Italy.

No wonder the Normans thought God was on their side. No door could be closed against them. They could walk in anywhere and take over. In reality the Normans were not, as they liked to think, unique. Their story is simply a dramatic example of changes creeping over Europe. The eleventh and twelfth centuries are a crucial period in European history. For the first time since plague hit the late Roman empire the population was expanding and was to go on expanding until cut back again by the Black Death. Waste land was being brought into cultivation, marshes drained, towns and trade developing rapidly. The Germans were colonising the Slav lands in eastern Europe. In Spain the Moslems were being rolled back and new Christian kingdoms formed. The population growth was sustained by improving the productivity of agriculture. What made that possible was a shift in the climate. For a couple of centuries western Europe was a little warmer and much drier. This benefited the north more than the south, which became too dry. It especially benefited grain production: wheat for bread, barley for beer, oats for horses. But to exploit the possibilities peasant labour had to be redeployed to produce surpluses for the market. The new unit of estate organisation was what we call the 'manor'. Control over land – and not simply over men – then

THE PEOPLE OF IRELAND

became critical to the power of lords. So they changed from the old practice of dividing up an inheritance among sons to having just one take over the whole. And instead of giving land to their vassals, they leased it in return for oaths of homage and military service.. This greater stability in landholding and the concentration of power in fewer hands was part of a trend towards a tighter organisation of society, and the transformation of loose groupings of peoples into disciplined states managed by effective central authorities. Organisation and discipline were the new watchwords. Monasteries – hitherto separate communities – were organised into monastic orders. Bishoprics – hitherto virtually autonomous – were being brought under central control. The fighting men had to learn new techniques of warfare: what counted was no longer acts of individual valour but the co-ordinated cavalry charge, hard to master but devastating in its effects. The upsurge of the new Europe is seen not merely in Norman exploits but in the Crusades. The First Crusade at the end of the eleventh century set up Europe's first colonies overseas, in the Holy Land. The Normans were deeply involved in that, sending contingents both from Normandy and southern Italy. As the crusaders made their way to Jerusalem the Normans seized control of Antioch and held on to it. Is it significant that there was never an Irish contingent on the Crusades?

The explanation for the sudden transformation of Normandy in the eleventh century into a tightly run mini-state is that its dukes latched on to the possibility of change very early and deliberately promoted it. The Normans became the most skilled practitioners of cavalry warfare. Heavily armoured knights were the battle tanks of the middle ages. They were enormously expensive to equip and maintain; but a few knights could get the better of hundreds of footsoldiers, so armies could be smaller and more mobile. But having won land it had to be held, so along with the knight went the castle. The typical French castle of the time was a stone tower. The Normans developed a simpler alternative which could be erected quickly with unskilled labour – not so much a castle as a fort. The technique was to dig a deep, wide circular ditch, throw up the earth to form a mound in the middle, put a watchtower of logs on the top, and link it to a stockaded enclosure where horses and supplies could be safeguarded. Such a fort was not impregnable, but a few men could hold out long

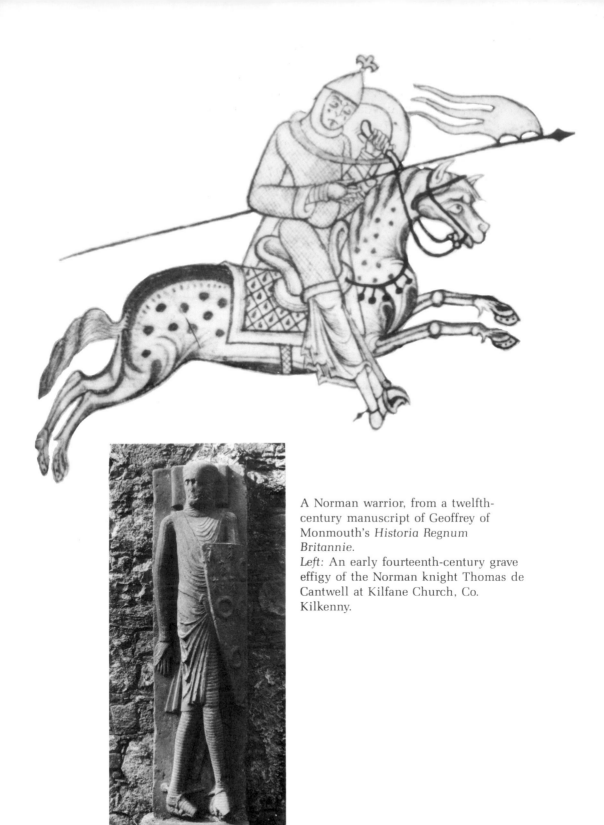

A Norman warrior, from a twelfth-century manuscript of Geoffrey of Monmouth's *Historia Regnum Britannie*.
Left: An early fourteenth-century grave effigy of the Norman knight Thomas de Cantwell at Kilfane Church, Co. Kilkenny.

enough for help to arrive. Once opposition had been cowed, a more imposing stone castle could be built as a residence and administrative centre, a town with a market encouraged to grow up round it, a monastery established. Military strength, commerce, and God-fearing piety were the mainstays of Norman power.

Rulers remote from the centres of change who nevertheless wished to modernise their realm, to stabilise it, and make their authority effective, could buy in expertise. This is what happened in Scotland. David I, king of Scots from 1124 to 1153 invited Normans from England to settle in Scotland in considerable numbers. He was careful to settle them on crown lands or where he had troublesome opponents. They did not displace the Scottish aristocracy but were slotted in alongside it. Of course the Normans were dependent on the king's patronage and so steadfastly loyal. They provided the essential underpinning to the monarchy while David set about modernising his kingdom. He introduced reformed monastic orders, set up new market towns, issued the first Scottish coinage, and reorganised his government along the lines of Norman England, with sheriffs and justices. His successors followed his example and by the end of the twelfth century Scotland had become a more or less typical European-style kingdom, with a mixed but remarkably stable society.

Why did that not happen in Ireland? It nearly did. There were some attempts at 'modernisation' from early in the twelfth century. Plans were drawn up for reorganising the bishoprics on the standard European model; but actually establishing the new bishoprics was very slow and frequently stalled altogether. The problem was that there was no one behind whom those who wanted change could rally to impose reform. In Scotland by David I's day there was only one king, and provincial rulers had become his subordinates. In Ireland there were many kings; effective power was still in the hands of province kings not the High King, and not even the province kings had undisputed authority. Vested interests in the old order were so deep rooted that any change seemed tantamount to a revolution. Any attempt to concentrate authority in kings and bishops threatened to undermine the influence of clan chieftains, local holy men and the traditional law-minders who were the guardians of custom.

One of the keenest 'modernisers', Dermot MacMurrough, king

of Leinster, provoked so much opposition that for a time he was thrown out. So he did what the king of Scots had done and sought permission from the king of England to recruit Normans to under-pin his kingship. Those who first came were few but they did the job of pacifying Leinster so effectively that King Dermot thought to make himself king of Ireland. For that he needed more Normans but had difficulty getting them. The notion of a 'Norman invasion' is a myth. Eventually he recruited the lord of Pembroke, Richard de Clare, usually known by his nickname of 'Strongbow'. Dermot bribed him by offering him his daughter in marriage and Leinster as his inheritance. It was a mistake. When the king of England heard about it he was furious. When Dermot died the High King, Rory O'Connor, king of Connaught tried to throw Strongbow out. He failed. His army was routed on the banks of the Liffey. That meant that the king of England had to intervene. He did not mind the Normans taking service under an Irish king, but now they were taking over. This was not like the Normans in Scotland, which is what he had expected; it was like the Normans in south-ern Italy, who were a menace to their neighbours. He did not want another Sicily on his doorstep.

So King Henry II moved in. The Normans accepted his over-lordship, and so did the Irish kings. There was no campaign against the Irish. Henry II had no intention of conquering Ireland; he wanted to stop the Normans doing it. He made a treaty with the High King by which he was to have charge of the Normans and Rory was to mind the Irish. This, however, was only a stop-gap. Partition was not a lasting answer to the problem. The proper answer was to have one authority in Ireland which could hold the balance of power and keep everyone in order. Henry did not wish to do it himself. Significantly he never included Ireland among his lordships. He was king of England, duke of Normandy, count of Anjou and duke of Aquitaine. That is how he styled himself. Ireland was not a welcome acquisition; it was a nuisance. His plan for Ireland was to move in one of his sons to take charge. That is what he did for his other dominions; each of his sons was assigned a portion to make his own. He did not break his treaty with the High King, but when Rory died and the high kingship lapsed he sent over his youngest son, John, with a support group of experienced administrators to establish a central authority. The intention was to set up a new kingdom of Ireland quite separate from the kingdom of England. Henry obtained a crown for the purpose from the papacy. But John was never actually crowned king of Ireland. The unexpected happened. Henry II had four sons who reached manhood, but by accidents of death John, the youngest, succeeded to all his father's dominions and was crowned king of England. It was this accident which linked the two realms; and of course it undermined the intention to have in Ireland a resident ruler.

Was it absurd to think that Irish and Normans could live peaceably together as Scots and Normans did? Not at all. Some of the early Normans disappear from view; they took service under Irish rulers and Gaelicised their names. There was intermarriage at the highest level. Hugh de Lacy married a daughter of Rory O'Connor. William de Burgh married a daughter of Donnel Mor O'Brien, king of Thomond. Dermot MacCarthy, king of Desmond, married a daughter of Thomas Bluet. John himself conferred knighthood on the king of Thomond. He favoured Irishmen as bishops. He recommended the Irish bishop of Ferns to become archbishop of Cashel, but when the other bishops chose another Irishman instead he did not object.

Particularly instructive is what happened in Meath. When Henry II came to Ireland Meath had been without an undisputed ruler for twenty years and was in disorder. Henry II put in Hugh de Lacy to take charge (mainly to keep out Strongbow). Hugh strung a network of castles across it, and using all the standard techniques of Norman management turned it into the most peaceable and prosperous province of Ireland. He gained the respect of the Irish for fair dealing and keeping his word. We happen to have the accounts of the steward of Meath for 1212. He lists the produce of the manors of the lordship, totalling 20,000 bushels of corn from the winter sowing and 30,000 bushels of oats. He accounts for 906 oxen assigned to the plough teams on the manors, and for twice as many cattle, 1,926, mostly from renders by the Irish: 55 cows from the annual vent of O'Rourke, 200 cows from the Irish in the wardship of Gilbert d'Angulo, 293 cows from the tribute of O'Neill. A hundred cows had been recovered from the cattle-rustler MacMahon, and 32 of them returned to the betaghs of Kells (the betaghs were Irish peasants). MacMahon gave another 200 cows to have a hearing before the king's chief justice. The contrast between the arable of the manors and the cattle grazing in Irish hands is very striking. The lordship of Meath was a mixed society of sod-busters and ranchers. These are two different ways of life which, as we know from Western films, can lead to friction, but which can co-exist if all are under one lord who has the power to keep the peace and arbitrate disputes.

In 1210 John mounted a major campaign in Ireland – not against the Irish but against the Norman barons. The Irish cooperated with him; the king of Connaught sent his men to help John in the siege of Carrickfergus. Why? There had recently been a dangerous new development. In 1204 King John had lost Normandy to the king of France. The barons had to forfeit their estates there. Those who could looked to Ireland to make up their losses. It was not difficult; Ireland was by European standards underpopulated, underdeveloped, and underexploited. Those corn figures for Meath are significant. There were huge profits to be made from corn growing for the European market. The trail was blazed by the lord of Leinster who was now William Marshal. He was not one of those who made their home in Ireland. He acquired Leinster by marriage to Strongbow's heiress, but did not even visit it for seventeen years – until after he lost his estates in Normandy. He then constructed a deep water port at New Ross to ship out corn from his Leinster manors, and started evicting the Irish from lands suitable for arable farming. Very soon King John's representative in Ireland was having trouble with all the major barons. John took a firm line. He was lord of all Ireland; he was not simply patron of the Normans, the Irish were equally his subjects. The acceptance of his lordship by the Irish rested on tolerance and respect. So he came to Ireland and forced the great barons to submit and surrender their charters. But he had to change his tune. By 1212 he was in deep trouble with his barons in England. He needed the support of barons who could draw on resources from Ireland. They gave it to him: they backed him in the Magna Carta crisis, but they exacted a price – a free hand in Ireland and no nonsense about respecting the rights of the Irish. When King John died his son and heir was nine years old. The regency government was headed by William Marshal. It was he who issued that order to the governor of Ireland in 1217 that no Irishman was henceforth to be appointed to high ecclesiastical office.

So the era of trying to forge a united Ireland with both Irish and Norman components – in a similar way to Scotland – gave way to an era of colonial exploitation by absentee landlords who regarded their estates in Ireland as extensions of their estates in England, and shipped over peasants from the mainland to work their fields. They elbowed the Irish aside and took over all the land suitable for arable farming. There are in Ireland today many people who think of themselves as Irish but whose ancestors were French, or English, or Welsh, or Flemish. The settlers were very successful in the thirteenth century and have left an enduring legacy. They made Dublin a capital city and seat of government, with counties and officials such as coroners. They established a legal system which survives today, rooted in the English common law and Magna Carta. The first of the witnesses to Magna Carta was the archbishop of Canterbury, the second was the archbishop of Dublin. It is the period which sees the spread of towns deep into Ireland – Kilkenny and Athlone to name but two – and the flourishing of new seaports such as Drogheda and Carrickfergus.

In the fourteenth century, however, the settlers were in retreat. The area effectively controlled by the government in Dublin sharply contracted. It is described in the textbooks as the period of 'the Gaelic revival'. So in a sense it was. But let us not jump to conclusions. The first point to note is that it was not a simple struggle for supremacy between Irish and English influences. The two cultures had intermingled. The finest writer of poetry in the Irish language in the fourteenth century was a man descended from the earliest Norman settlers – Gerald FitzMaurice, third earl of Desmond. He was for a time the king of England's governor in Ireland. Those who had made their home in Ireland for five generations had become 'Anglo-Irish'. A Dublin chronicler of the fourteenth century speaks of them quite naturally as *populus Hibernie* – 'people of Ireland'. The leading families had Norman ancestors, but they had become as much a part of the fabric of society in Ireland as their descendants are today. They are the FitzGeralds, the Barrys, the Cogans and Wogans, the Roches, the Powers and the Burkes. Their counterparts among the Gaelic leaders imitated their life style and adopted imported methods. They built castles, they issued charters, they had seals, they gave themselves coats of arms, they used the king of England's coinage. One of their demands was to have English law extended to the whole of Ireland. In recovering lands from the settlers they were not recreating an Irish past. Many of them would have much preferred to become like English barons.

There is another point about the so-called 'Gaelic revival'. We

Though much restored, St Canice's Cathedral, Kilkenny, is a good example of Norman religious architecture.
Below: Garret Fitzgerald and Peter Barry, the two Irishmen most closely associated with the Anglo-Irish Agreement of 1985, bear the surnames of prominent Norman families.

should not suppose that it alone caused the contraction of the colonial settlement. To a large extent it was more a consequence than a cause. The economic boom which had sustained the expansion of western Europe for over two centuries had come to an end. The growth of population faltered, and was then savagely cut back by the plague known as the Black Death. Let us beware of looking at Irish history in a closed compartment. The medieval expansion of western Europe was over. It was retreating from the peripheries. The colonies in the Holy Land were abandoned. German colonial expansion in eastern Europe pulled back, leaving pockets of German settlers in Slav lands. Now there is an interesting parallel which no one has pursued.

6

The Scots

History and geography have combined to make Ulster almost as much a Scottish as an Irish province; the Scots have played an important role in shaping the life of the province, but they have, like other peoples, contributed their share of disharmony and conflict in Ireland.

Finlay Holmes

GEOGRAPHY and history have combined to link the peoples of what we now call Scotland and Ireland closely together. The Mull of Kintyre, which can be seen from Ireland on a clear day, is only twelve miles from the coast of Co. Antrim. Over the centuries, the narrow channel between the two countries has been a bridge for people and ideas moving in both directions.

Ireland's first inhabitants may have used that route to enter the island and, later, Scotland took its name from the *Scotti* – Latin for Irish – who, in the sixth century AD, extended their north-eastern kingdom of Dal Riata eastwards into what is now Argyll. The great monastery of *Candida Casa* – the 'White House' – in Galloway influenced the development of Irish monasticism, which, in turn, contributed to the evangelisation of Scotland through the community founded on Iona by Columba. The Irish, it has been said, gave the Scots their name, their language (Gaelic) and their Christianity. Thus, long before the seventeenth century and the Plantation of Ulster, Scotland and the north of Ireland were closely linked.

Viking invasions and settlements in the ninth and tenth centuries interrupted relations between the Scots and Irish, but, in the middle ages, Scottish mercenary soldiers, the formidable gallowglass, found a market for their martial skills in Ulster and settled easily among a kindred people. In the wake of Bannockburn in 1314, Edward Bruce, brother of Scotland's national hero, Robert, was crowned High King of Ireland, but his challenge to English rule in Ireland was short-lived. Another significant link between Scotland and Ulster was the arrival in 1399 of John Mor MacDonnell, Lord of Isla. He extended his Scottish patrimony into north Antrim through his marriage to Margery Bisset, heiress to the estates carved out by her Norman ancestors in the twelfth century. The MacDonnells proved to be stubborn survivors. In the sixteenth century, coming under increasing pressure from central government in Scotland, they began to expand their Irish interests, bringing in Scots tenants who found themselves very much at home among Ulster folk who spoke a variant of their own Gaelic language.

The English in Ireland viewed these developments with suspicion, however. In Mary Tudor's reign, when the strategy of colonisation by plantation was introduced in Ireland, there were plans to drive out these Scots and replace them with Welsh and northern English settlers. But the Scots were still there when Elizabeth I succeeded Mary. The Protestant archbishop of Armagh, Hugh Dowdell, advocated their expulsion as urgent government policy, 'so that they might never be able to continue or dwell therein'. This had still not been achieved when the accession of James VI of Scotland to the English throne in 1603 changed their prospects dramatically.

One of his early acts was to confirm an increased grant of land to Sir Randall MacDonnell. Among the new tenants whom this Catholic landowner introduced were Lowland Scots who were Protestants. They were the first of a new kind of Scottish immigrant and soon James began to grant land in Antrim and Down to Lowland Scots. He allowed two Ayrshire men, James Hamilton and Hugh Montgomery, to share in the dismemberment of the Co. Down estates of Conn O'Neill. O'Neill's part in the bargain was escape from prison in Carrickfergus and a pardon for his alleged crimes. The Crown's concern was that 'the sea coasts might be possessed by Scottish men who would be traders as proper to his majesty's future advantage'.

Thus began the free enterprise colonisation of Antrim and Down by Lowland Scots. It preceded and prepared the way for the later official colonisation of Armagh, Coleraine (now Londonderry), Cavan, Donegal, Fermanagh and Tyrone which is known as the

Plantation of Ulster. Monaghan had already been colonised by Englishmen and its Irish landholders brought into an English system of land tenure.

It is commonly believed that it was this official plantation of mid and west Ulster which established a permanent Scots presence in Ireland. In fact most of the Scots who came to Ulster in the seventeeth century came either to Antrim and Down or arrived in the second half of the century.

It was the success of the Scottish settlements in Antrim and Down which encouraged the Crown to embark upon the official plantation, following the so-called Flight of the Earls in 1607. The flight to Catholic Europe of the O'Neill, earl of Tyrone, and the O'Donnell, earl of Tyrconnell or Donegal, and about a hundred lesser chieftains, signalled their recognition that their long campaign to resist the advance of English authority and law in Ulster had failed. They could not face a future of diminishing independence and influence. Their military struggle in the last years of Elizabeth's reign had left Ulster devastated and depopulated, ripe for redevelopment. The Crown used the flight of the earls, whose estates were declared forfeit, to initiate a vast enterprise of colonisation and re-distribution of land in mid and west Ulster.

The Plantation of Ulster followed a number of precedents both in Ireland and in colonial America. Sixteenth-century plantations in Leix and Offaly and in Munster had lacked sufficient English tenant-farmers and artisans to ensure lasting stability. The Ulster plantation attracted, in addition to English and Welsh settlers, a substantial number of lowland Scots. It was not only landowners, a military aristocracy, who settled in Ulster, but farmers, masons, smiths and carpenters. The pattern had been established in Antrim and Down. The records of the Montgomery estates in Co. Down report that 'everybody minded their trades, and the plough, and the spade, building and setting fruit trees in orchards and gardens, and by ditching in their grounds.'

The settlements in Antrim and Down had not exhausted the supply of potential colonists among the Lowland Scots. 'Scotland,' claimed Sir William Alexander, founder of a colony in Nova Scotia, 'by reason of her populousnesse, being constrained to disburthen herself, like the painfull bees, did every yeere send forth swarmes.' In the Scottish Lowlands there was a surplus both of population and, in some hands, of capital. Scotsmen had been settling in Europe, as far away as Poland, and there had been unsuccessful attempts to colonise the western highlands and islands. Now Ulster, with cheap land on good terms under the protection of the English Crown, offered attractive possibilities for the upwardly mobile and for those who urgently needed to repair declining fortunes or make a fresh start.

Propaganda for the plantation claimed that there was abundant land for both immigrants and the existing population. Many of the latter remained to find that the new order was less oppressive than the old, for chieftains like the O'Neill had had few scruples about overriding the Gaelic traditions which they championed when it suited their own interests. Of course there were also those who resented the arrival of what one of their poets called 'an impure swarme of foreigners, an excommunicated rabble of Saxons and Scotsmen'. They retreated to the forests and hills, finding refuges from which to harass the settlers while waiting and hoping for the restoration of the old order.

The immigrants were well aware that these 'wood-kerne', as they called them, 'do threaten every house, if opportunity of time and place afford'. Some of them were forced to live and work, 'with sword in one hand and axe in the other'. The fact that they established their communities under conditions of continual insecurity, with their settlements threatened with destruction in the 1640s, and later in 1688-9, contributed to their wary, self-reliant frontiersmen's outlook. This was to find its permanently evocative myth in the siege of Derry.

It was not race – Scottish planter and Ulster Irishman shared the same mixed race – but religion, which was to separate the planter from the Gael. Not all Scots settlers were Presbyterians; some were Roman Catholics, others were Episcopalians who became bishops in the Church of Ireland. Not all Presbyterians were Scots, some were English Puritans and there are enough older Irish names among later Presbyterians to indicate that some of the exisiting population found their spiritual home in the Presbyterian congregations which the settlers established. Undoubtedly it was the Presbyterianism which the settlers brought to Ireland which gave their communities cohesion and permanence. The structures, doctrines and discipline of Presbyterianism contributed to their self-awareness as a distinctive people – a people of God. Terence Brown has suggested that the

This mid-seventeenth-century 'barn church' at Ballinderry, Co. Antrim, is one of the few remaining examples of church architecture from the Plantation period. Much of its timber furnishings came from the surrounding historic oakwoods of Killultagh. *Left:* The Scots brought their own architectural styles. Ballygally Castle in Co. Antrim is a near-perfect example of a seventeenth-century Scottish tower house.

metrical psalms, which provided the worship song of Presbyterianism, were peculiarly appropriate for a settler people to take as their spiritual and artistic staple. Their blend of agrarian, pastoral imagery with a rhetoric of warfare and survival amidst ungodly enemies must have provided the Presbyterian settlers with an interpretative myth of their own experience in the fertile valleys of their promised land, wrested from the Canaanites.

The south-west of Scotland, from which many of the settlers came, was a stronghold of radical Presbyterianism. Some of the founding fathers of the kirk in Ulster, men like Robert Blair of Bangor and John Livingstone of Killinchy, were leaders in Scotland of the Scottish campaign of resistance to Episcopacy and Erastianism. Another powerful influence in determining the character of Irish Presbyterianism was the vivid experience of religious revival which accompanied its beginnings in Co. Antrim, anticipating similar experiences on the frontier in colonial America.

The Presbyterianism of the Scots settlers made them dissenters in Ireland, bringing disabilities and even mild persecution – their services of worship, church courts and marriages were deemed illegal, and they had to pay tithes and church rates to support the Protestant established church – and this experience injected bitterness into a people already hard.

The defection to the establishment of many of their gentry, for whom conformity and escape from the discipline of kirk sessions were attractive, increased their sturdy independence and lack of deference to rank and station. Some of Ulster's most distinguished aristocratic families like the Londonderrys were originally Scottish and Presbyterian, as were the forbears of Sarah Ferguson, duchess of York.

Although many of the first Scottish settlers were killed or driven away in the Irish rebellion of 1641 – though nothing like the 50,000 which contemporary propagandists claimed – their numbers were more than replenished by later waves of immigration, particularly after the Williamite victory of 1690. Londonderry rivalled Carrickfergus and Donaghadee as a port of entry. The Foyle basin, known as 'The Laggan', embracing north-west Tyrone and east Donegal, became, with Antrim and Down, the chief areas of Scottish settlement. It is difficult to be precise about numbers; contemporary statistics tend to be overestimates. The combined English and Scots population in the census of 1659 was 40,000. It has been estimated that another 50,000 Scots settled in Ulster during the remainder of the seventeenth century.

Their Presbyterianism kept their links with Scotland alive and strong. Until higher education became available in Belfast in the nineteenth century and they established their own theological colleges in Belfast and Londonderry, their ministers were trained in the Scottish universities. The close links between Irish Presbyterians and their mother church in Scotland led to the appearance in Ireland of the great divisions in Scottish Presbyterianism. Seceders of different kinds and Covenanters, who believed that the great Covenants of the seventeenth century were permanently binding contracts with God and could not be modified or set aside, found support in Ireland. Their Old Light Calvinism was more popular with rural congregations than the New Light Liberalism of some Irish Presbyterian ministers. Significantly, in the nineteenth century, when the victory of Henry Cooke's Old Light party in the synod of Ulster, the mainstream Irish Presbyterian body, made union with the Seceders possible in 1840, the new united Presbyterian Church in Ireland took sides with the Free Kirk, rather than with the Church of Scotland in the great Scottish Disruption of 1843. These continuing links with Scotland tended to preserve the distinctive identity of the descendants of Scots settlers in Ulster. A French visitor to Ireland at the end of the eighteenth century described Belfast as having 'completely the look of a Scotch town and the character of its inhabitants shows considerable resemblance to that of the people of Glasgow'. A generation later, in 1839, another Frenchman observed that Ulster was 'the Scotland of Ireland', characterised by the 'ancient anti-catholic prejudice which its inhabitants had brought with them as colonists of James I'.

It would be wrong, however, to give the impression that the descendants of Scottish settlers in Ulster remained permanent aliens in Ireland. Undoubtedly the original seventeenth-century settlers had been cast in the role of agents of the British interest in Ireland, a role later recognised by the Crown payment of *regium donum* – 'royal bounty' – for Presbyterian ministers, in spite of the fact that they were dissenters. But if some aspects of their experience in Ireland, as in 1641 and in 1689-90, encouraged them to continue in that role, other aspects made them increasingly

Scots dissenters suffered disabilities and even persecution at the hands of the Protestant establishment, both in Scotland and Ireland. This Scottish painting of a Covenanters baptism mirrors the 'hedge schools' and outdoor Masses of Irish Catholic tradition.

dissatisfied with their lot in Ireland. They became opponents, rather than allies, of the English Protestant establishment.

To their disabilities as dissenters were added, in rural areas, the tensions of the landlord/tenant farmer relationship. Most landlords were members of the established church, most Presbyterians were tenant farmers. In times of economic recession, with rising rents and falling prices, life became a struggle for survival. As early as 1636 some ministers led an unsuccessful expedition to colonial America, following the example of the English Pilgrim Fathers. In the 1680s Francis Makemie and other Ulster Presbyterian ministers, mostly from the Laggan presbytery in the west of the province, became the founding fathers of American Presbyterianism. In the eighteenth century what had been a trickle of Ulster Scots emigrants to America became a flood. Thousands, impelled largely by economic motives, abandoned Ireland for the New World. Some of them became determined supporters of the American colonists' campaign for independence from Britain. Their experience and example had important repercussions among those who remained in Ireland. The philosophy of the American colonists – as expressed in their famous Declaration of Independence – that all men had inalienable rights to life, liberty and the pursuit of happiness, had explosive implications for eighteenth-century Ireland.

Such ideas were characteristic of the eighteenth-century Enlightenment which was exposing the privileges and injustice of the archaic political and social systems of the old order in Europe to rational scrutiny and criticism. Some Ulster Scots imbibed these ideas as students in the Scottish universities; more as members of popular local reading societies. Inspired by events in America and in France they became involved in a movement for radical reform in Ireland. It was in the 'Scotch town' of Belfast that the first society of United Irishmen was formed in 1791. Its plan was to unite all Irishmen, 'Protestant, Roman Catholic and Dissenter', to achieve revolutionary change in Ireland – a democratic parliament, full civil rights for all, irrespective of religion, and an end to English domination. It was the brainchild of a graduate of the universities of Glasgow and Edinburgh, William Drennan, and its first members were sons of the manse and elders of the kirk.

But it was only some of the Ulster Scots who glimpsed the

United Irish vision – an *avante garde* in Belfast and in counties Antrim and Down – and the rebellion which they led in 1798 was as much an expression of long-standing Presbyterian and peasant grievances as a revolutionary crusade. The tragedy of 1798 was that what the United Irishmen *intended* to be a crusade for Irish liberty and against injustice became a civil war with Irishmen fighting Irishmen. If descendants of Scots settlers fought as rebels in counties Antrim and Down they were also prominent in the ranks of the yeomanry in Fermanagh, Tyrone, Derry and Armagh.

Subsequent Irish history might seem to suggest that Ulster Scot participation in the United Irish movement was only a temporary aberration from their permanent role as supporters of the British interest in Ireland – the one occasion when Ulster joined Ireland. But that would not be the whole truth. There is truth also in the contention that, in the nineteenth century, Ireland left Ulster, that the non-sectarian vision of the United Irishmen was replaced by a Roman Catholic and Gaelic Irish nationalism which excluded the aggressively Protestant Ulster Scots who were beginning to believe that their economic interests were bound up with those of the north of England and west of Scotland in whose industrial revolution Belfast had begun to share.

The traditional grievances of the Ulster Scots had been largely removed in the nineteenth century with the destruction of the political and economic power of the landlords and the disestab-lishment of the Church of Ireland. Their political aspirations were beginning to be satisfied with their achievement of full civil rights. They welcomed the inceasing liberalisation and democratisation of the structures of British politics. They thought of themselves not as Scots but as Irish and British. Two hundred years of Irish soil and climate had made them Irish. Eighteenth-century Ulster Scots emigrants to southern Pennsylvania gave their new townships Ulster rather than Scottish names – Antrim, Armagh, Derry, Fermanagh and Tyrone. At the end of the nineteenth cen-tury J. J. Shaw, a Greyabbey-born academic and lawyer, in an open letter to another Ulster Scot explained why, though proud of his Irishness and of United Irish ancestors, he opposed Gladstone's policy of giving Ireland home rule to satisfy Irish nationalist demands:

> If you and I are not Irishmen, I do not know who can be entitled to the name. Eight generations of your ancestors and of mine

sleep beneath the shadow of the old Abbey walls. These men through their several generations were born and lived and died in Ireland. Every morning they went forth to their work and to their labour till the evening. They spent their days and their strength and their substance on Irish soil. They subdued the earth and planted it. The wilderness and the solitary place were glad for them; and they made the desert to rejoice and blossom as the rose. There is not a square yard round the places where we were born which does not bear the marks of their industry and care.

But their Irishness was not the anti-British Irishness of some of their nationalist contemporaries. A moderator of the Irish Presbyterian General Assembly, speaking not long after Shaw had published his open letter on the Home Rule question, could claim without fear of contradiction:

Seldom, if ever, have any of us been ashamed to declare that we are Britons. . . whatever our views of the best solution to the Irish problem, the sentiment of loyalty towards and pride in the British inheritance and commonwealth of peoples has been common to us all.

Significantly, his statement has been quoted and endorsed by two historians of Irish Presbyterianism, Ernest Davey and J. M. Barkley, writing in 1940 and 1960 respectively. A majority of the descendants of Scottish settlers in Ulster would still see no contradiction in being both Irish and British. Another moderator of the Irish General Assembly, T. M. Johnstone, was probably right when he claimed, 'If in one sense Ulstermen are Irishmen first and Britishers afterwards, in another sense they are Ulstermen first and Irishmen afterwards.'

What has been the contribution of Scottish immigrants to Ireland? Like other peoples, the Ulster Scots have a somewhat self-admiring historical myth about their contribution to Irish life. There were echoes of it in the words I have quoted from J. J. Shaw but it was enunciated resonantly by the Reverend Henry Cooke, one of its most eloquent exponents, addressing the General Assembly of the Church of Scotland in 1836:

Our Scottish forefathers were planted in the most barren portions of our lands – the most rude and lawless of the provinces

Henry Cooke (1788–1868), a dominant force in the development of
nineteenth-century Presbyterianism in that 'most rude and lawless of the
provinces'.

– Scottish industry has drained its bogs and cultivated its barren wastes; substituted towns and cities for its hovels and clachans and given peace and good order to a land of confusion and blood.

Like most such myths it contains elements of truth, as does the alternative Irish nationalist myth which portrays the Scots as greedy robbers of the best Irish land.

Scots immigrants have stamped their personality upon much of Ulster and have penetrated to all parts of Ireland. Scottish influence is still audible in some Ulster dialects and a vocabulary loaded with words like 'skunner', 'gunk', 'sleekit' and 'girn'. Scottish industry has brought prosperity to parts of Ulster but not to its bogs and barren wastes. The Scots did not introduce any revolutionary agricultural methods or implements though their two-eared Scotch spade gave the Irish the expression 'digging with the wrong foot'. Later came Scotch carts, ploughs and threshing machines. When the north-east of Ireland was relatively prosperous there were those who attributed that prosperity, and the success of the industries which provided it, to the Calvinism and special talents of the descendants of Scots settlers. Less is heard of such ideas in a period of economic decline. Geography and the emergence of entrepreneurs of genius like Harland and Wolff – neither of them Ulster Scots – had more to do with nineteenth-century industrial success than religion or race. Yet, as a modern Scottish historian has observed, 'it is impossible not to suspect that Calvinist seriousness of purpose had some effect on both intellectual and economic life.'

As well as good farmers and businessmen the Ulster Scots have produced good doctors, teachers, preachers and engineers. If they have produced little great literature, their eighteenth-century vernacular poets can stand comparison with Burns himself. Perhaps inevitably, their best writers and scholars, like Helen Waddell and Lord Kelvin, have found fame outside Ireland. Their good grammar schools and Belfast's university, which, in its early days, owed much to Scottish models, reflect their respect for education. They have built neat, functional homes but few fine buildings, though John Wesley described the meeting-house of Belfast's First Presbyterian congregation as 'the completest place of public worship I have ever seen'.

Commonly caricatured as a gloomy and silent bigot, the Ulster

Scot is recognised by those who know him well as a loyal friend with a mordant sense of humour, critical of human pretensions and self-importance. He has not, as Henry Cooke claimed, 'brought peace and good order to a land of confusion and blood'; instead he has contributed his share to disharmony and conflict in Ireland, if only because he cannot compromise what he believes to be sacred principle, which others may see as self-interest. It may be significant that when, earlier this century, he sought a symbol with which to focus and express his opposition to Irish Home Rule, he found it in the great Scottish Covenants of the seventeenth century, originally devised to safeguard the purity of the Reformation in Scotland and in the British Isles. History and geography have combined to make Ulster as much a Scottish as an Irish province.

7

The English

The early Anglo-Norman settlers in Ireland seemed English to the Irish and Irish to the English: centuries later their predicament remained unresolved and the colonial community continued to grapple with the difficulties of maintaining satisfactory relations with a mother country that went on changing.

Aidan Clarke

M Y subject is a large one, and I will qualify it at the outset by choosing as my text some words spoken by Maurice Fitzgerald when he rallied his men outside Dublin in 1170, at the very beginning of the history of the first English colony in Ireland: 'Just as we are English to the Irish,' he told them, 'so we are Irish to the English.' A large part of my theme will be to show how time seemed to prove Fitzgerald right, as the colony that he helped to found in the twelfth century was itself conquered five centuries later. In speaking as he did, however, Fitzgerald was drawing attention to two misunderstandings. Just as the English were perverse in thinking of his men as Irish, so the Irish were wrong in regarding them as English. Some were English, of course, but others were Norman, Welsh and Fleming. They had a great deal more in common with one another than they had with the native Irish: they shared the same legal principles, economic practices, property laws and social conventions, and they acknowledged a common political authority, but they were culturally disparate nonetheless, and their experiences in Ireland were not such as to unify them. To understand the nature of what was to come, it is first necessary to understand that the Englishness of the early colonists was not something that they brought with them to Ireland, but something that their descendants acquired over time and in varying degrees.

These degrees of variation were influenced both by the character of the settlement and by the nature of the conquest. Settlement was fragmented. There was dense colonisation around the points of disembarkation, at Dublin and the south-east. From there, the settlers radiated out, along the river valleys and the low ground to the south, the west and the north-east, thinning out along the lines of advance, not over-running the Irish, but displacing them and pushing them aside. They settled the fertile ground, staying below the 200-metre line everywhere, and controlling the river system which was the key to the command of communications. The pattern that emerged was made up of a colonial heartland in Leinster, which came to be known as the Pale, and which was connected with numerous and extensive clusters of outlying settlements scattered among the Irish. As time went on, however, the Irish recovered ground, notably in the early fourteenth century. In the midlands as well as further afield, they over-ran the weaker settlements and flowed around the stronger ones, breaking the lines of communication and isolating the colonies both from one another and from the heartland. That Gaelic resurgence was short-lived. Tensions diminished after the visitation of plague known as the Black Death struck in the middle of the fourteenth century and sharply reduced the population, leaving plenty of resources for the survivors and removing any need to fight for them. For the remainder of the medieval period, colonist and native each had room to expand within their own areas, but the geography of colonial Ireland remained as it had been when the Black Death came – dispersed and disconnected.

The dynamics of the invasion itself contributed to that development. The Norman invasion was a private enterprise operation. The settlements were established by freebooting adventurers whose activities were uncoordinated and uncontrolled, and largely remained so. The Crown did assert its jurisdiction over those of its subjects who had gone to Ireland. It demanded obedience and taxes from them, and it acknowledged an obligation to provide them with basic government services, but it did not claim the Irish as its subjects. Ireland was a lordship, not a kingdom. In practice, the kings of England had neither the will nor the power to exert authority over more than the heartland. Even there, the crown's presence was little more than token and, in truth, its failure to undertake the defence of the colony deprived it of the moral right to require more than token obedience.

The colonists were left to fend for themselves in an only partly conquered Ireland, and their responses were diverse. Each settler community developed the strategy of survival that best suited its own local circumstances. The most remote settlers, in places like Kerry and Mayo, went native, adopting Gaelic customs, Gaelic speech, and even gaelicised family names, but their hibernicisation stopped short of assimilation, if only because their Gaelic host society, structured as it was on ancestral relationships, never lost sight of their origins. Less distant or better organised communities of settlers, on the borders of the Pale or in the powerful lordships of Desmond and Ormond in the south-west and the south-midlands, adapted more complexly, perhaps more calculatedly, mingling Gaelic practices with their inherited ways and developing a frontier style of life from which they were able to draw the maximum autonomy, notionally acknowledging but rarely respecting the authority of a king who was unable to protect them. In the counties around Dublin and in the major towns and their immediate hinterlands the position was very different: there, the settlers benefited from the goverment's legal, administrative and military services; they kept in close touch with England, where the sons of both landed and merchant families often finished their education, and they resisted local influences. As England itself changed, they changed with it; acquiring the English language, setting up a parliament, incorporating legal and institutional modifications as they evolved in the mother country, following fashion. Over time, in short, they became what they had not been at the outset: they became English. But they remained conscious of the reality that differences of situation prevented them from being accepted as wholly English. At the beginning of the fourteenth century they still displayed that same sense of aggrieved distinctiveness that Maurice Fitzgerald had expressed 250 years earlier, and they spoke of themselves as 'the middle nation'.

Their attitudes have been commonly misinterpreted. They were not cultural imperialists. Far from trying to impose their system upon the Irish, they jealously reserved its benefits for themselves. The policies for which they are best known, the successive acts of parliament which were codified as the Statutes of Kilkenny in 1366, which banned intermarriage with the Irish, prohibited land-leasing arrangements with them, curtailed trade and debarred Gaelic clergy from livings in the Pale, were measures of containment, anxious rather than arrogant in tone, designed to protect settlers from the Gaelic influences to which many had already succumbed rather than to discriminate against the Irish. The other problem created by their position in the 'middle' was tackled in a less celebrated law which noted the hostility between Englishmen born in England and Englishmen born in Ireland and made it an offence for them to call one another 'English hobby' or 'Irish dog'. It was already too late to halt hibernicisation beyond the Pale, just as it was also futile to hope that legal sanctions could suppress the sense that the settlers were not the same as the native English. Even the native Irish were careful to make that distinction: to them, the settlers, whether they were hibernicised or not, were the Gall; the English born in England were the Sasanagh. And the anglicised Palesmen and townsmen, contemptuous of the degeneracy of the outlying settlers though they were, never ceased to think of them as part of their own stock.

In important respects, the colony in Ireland was autonomous. That was not, however, a unique position. Medieval governments were not interventionist. Throughout England itself government was in the hands of the leaders of powerful landed families who were expected to make as few calls as possible on central government and who only became accountable when things went seriously wrong. In the same way, Ireland was ruled increasingly from within. The kings discharged their duties by appointing prominent settler magnates to act as viceroys and these men, combining royal authority with their own resources, undertook responsibility for administering and protecting the Pale. That task involved them in what amounted to the management of diplomatic relations with the Irish and colonial lordships, and the discretion they exercised was very wide. By the end of the medieval period this delegated control seemed close to becoming a hereditary perquisite of the earls of Kildare. At the same time, however, it was reaching the end of its usefulness.

Kildare had his supporters, of course, but autonomy was far from having the undivided approval of the Pale community. Many believed that Kildare's ascendancy came between them and their king, and compromised their rights as subjects; many were deeply dissatisfied with the limited scope of government authority in Ireland; they were convinced that their future security and prosperity depended upon its being enlarged, and they suspected that Kildare had a vested interest in the confused and dangerous *status*

Kilteel Castle, Co. Kildare, one of the many towers built to protect English settlements against incursions from beyond the Pale.

quo. Two things gave them hope at the beginning of the sixteenth century. One was the assertive character of the new Tudor kingship; they watched noble power and privilege being brought under restraint in England and hoped that the crown might be persuaded to assert itself in the same way in Ireland. The other was a change in their own way of approaching political problems, one that they learned from Renaissance humanism. Medieval fatalism was replaced by a belief that men might reasonably try to improve their condition, that governments had a duty to take initiatives and tackle problems. The plan of action that the Palesmen now began to urge upon the government was simple, but profound. Ireland should cease to be a feudal fief and become a kingdom; the Irish should be brought within the law, welcomed as the king's subjects and induced to abandon their traditional way of life. Instead, they should till the ground, live in settled communities, adopt English property law, and obey the authority of the state. They should renounce 'barbarism' and embrace 'civility'. The words themselves reveal a new perspective. In the past, the Irish had been seen in a matter of fact way as different. Now they were seen in more sophisticated yet more simplistic terms as a primitive people, whose manner of life reflected the fact that they were still at an early age of social evolution. What was proposed was a programme that would help them to jump the evolutionary gap. There was no altruism in this; what the Palesmen aimed at was their own greater security in an Ireland newly 'made English' (as the phrase had it), and ruled by themselves.

Their plan was frustrated by the combined impact of Protestant reform and English expansionism. When Henry VIII overthrew Kildare and set up a system of direct rule in 1534, he was not doing the bidding of the Palesmen; he was making sure that Ireland could be effectively defended against European retaliation for the divorce of his Spanish wife. And when he accepted the kingship of Ireland from the Irish parliament in 1541 he did so because he needed to rebut the argument that since the lordship of Ireland had been formally approved by the papacy, his authority there was at the pope's discretion.

The slow completion of the conquest of Ireland that Henry thus more or less inadvertently initiated was a confused process. From the outset, there were alternative possibilities. The country might be brought under control through the anglicisation of its people, as the Palesmen urged and the government itself accepted in principle, but that was a protracted and uncertain way. Alternatively, it might be conquered outright and control assured by the importation of new English colonists, but that was costly and difficult. These competing policies were favoured by rival interest groups. The 'English of Irish birth', as they were clumsily called, were sure that the conciliation of the Irish was most conducive to the welfare and safety of their descendents. The 'English of English birth' were either short-stay officials, unconcerned with the long run, or adventurers who had nothing to gain from the conversion of the *status quo* into a quiescent community under the Crown. The competition was an unequal one for two reasons. First, the Crown's policy in Ireland was ultimately governed by international pressure rather than by local conditions, and force always superseded conciliation in times of foreign crisis when defence became the overriding priority. Secondly, the 'English of Irish birth' were still 'a middle nation', distrusted and resented by newcomers from England. As early as the 1550s, a Protestant reformer struck a new and prophetic note when, having referred in conventional terms to the natives as the 'wild Irish', he went on to speak of newcomers like himself as 'people of our nation', and to dismiss the colonial community as 'the tame Irish'. Those who followed him to Ireland were envious of the entrenched position of the colonists and found credible grounds for disparaging them in their failure to follow England in embracing the Protestant religion. That disparagement met with an understanding response in England itself, where the interest in Ireland was largely strategic. In a Europe now divided by religion, the first line of English defence was effective control over Ireland. It was obvious both that control must be in Protestant hands and that the more Protestant Ireland became the more secure it would be. Again, there were alternative possibilities; the Irish could be converted to Protestantism, or authentic English Protestants could be brought to Ireland to transform it. And again, the first of these possibilities was slow and uncertain. So migration was encouraged, the expropriation of Irish land was facilitated and, as opportunity offered, the systematic colonisation of selected areas – the process that contemporaries called 'plantation' – was undertaken.

The elaboration of plantation schemes brought a series of rapid decisions about the status of the historic colonists. In the first, in

O Sydney worthy of tryple re-
nowne,
For plagyng the traytours that
troubled the crowne. 1581.

The Aldermen of Dublin, in full regalia, assemble to greet Lord Deputy
Sidney as he returns from a campaign against the rebellious Irish.

the midland counties of Leix and Offaly in the 1550s, arrangements were made to screen applications for land grants from local settlers, so that those of doubtful loyalty or insufficient Englishness could be excluded. By this stage, the government was making a working distinction between 'the queen's loyal subjects' in the heartland and the towns and 'the queen's English rebels' in the outlying rural areas. In the second major scheme, in Munster in the 1580s, only those born in England were eligible. In a single generation, in short, the Palesmen had been downgraded. In the 1540s, they had been partners of the Crown in a new experiment in Irish government: in the 1580s, they were judged unfit for trust. Beyond the Pale, developments were more extreme. As the government gradually asserted its authority over the outlying areas, it paid particular attention to the degenerate colonists whose reclamation to civility and obedience became a special priority. The Irish could scarcely be held responsible for their barbarism; the settlers had embraced it by choice. And they were not only the more culpable, but the more vulnerable. Nominally, they held their lands from the Crown and had no recourse if the Crown should take them back to bestow upon more deserving subjects, as it showed every sign of intending to do. Obstinately, they resisted the extension of crown control, to the point of resorting to arms in Munster. It was the lands of the Geraldine earl of Desmond and his settler followers that were confiscated for plantation in the 1580s, not the lands of the native Irish. The old, unsatisfactory colony was to be replaced by a new one.

The final crisis of the 1590s, when the government, against a background of international conflict, completed the conquest by subduing Ulster, brought divided responses. The ancestral loyalties of the Palesmen held firm; they fought with the government, seizing the chance to show that their Catholicism did not in any way diminish their allegiance to the Crown. Elsewhere, as ever, the settlers acted as their local interests dictated; some fought for the crown, and some against it; some did both, and others, particularly in the towns, tried to maintain a safe and profitable neutrality.

Thus it was that when the war ended in English victory the problems posed by the historic colony remained unresolved. The government interpreted its success as a Protestant triumph and moved quickly to enforce religious discrimination. The Palesmen resisted, strenuously affirming that their Englishness and their record of loyalty placed them among the conquerors, not among the conquered. The colonial communities elsewhere hastily rediscovered their historic identity, resurrected their historic surnames where necessary, and allied themselves with the Pale against government policy, insisting that their Catholicism was perfectly compatible with loyalty and that they were entitled to be treated as Englishmen. For the first time, the colonial communities united, with the degenerate colonists shedding their own past and claiming to share the political and cultural traditions of the Palesmen. Collectively, they adopted the name 'Old English', to stress both their origins and their prior rights against the recent Protestant settlers, whom they called the 'New English'. These Old English made up a formidable interest. Between them, they owned more than a third of Irish land, and a much higher proportion of the best land; and they largely controlled Irish trade. The government was uncertain how to deal with them. It was unwilling to trust them, but unable to suppress them, and it soon realised that what the situation required was more New English to balance the Old English.

The opportunity to make progress came almost at once, with the flight of the Ulster earls to the continent. The decision to colonise the province was taken not merely as a means of pacifying that part of Ireland, but also as a way of introducing a sufficiently large block of Protestant upholders of the government to allow military victory to be converted into political control. In the years that followed, further colonising opportunities were provided in the midlands, at the expense of the Irish; plans were made to plant Connacht, at the expense of both Old English and Irish; and the migration of English settlers to all parts of Ireland was actively encouraged. Although the Old English managed to hold their own, their attempts to secure guarantees of their position were unsuccessful and it was clear that time was not on their side. Inexorably, they were being challenged, disadvantaged and threatened with the ultimate penalty for their Catholicism, the loss of their land.

It was, of course, open to them to change their religion, but the threat that they faced was not exclusively religious. The England that conquered Ireland was not only Protestant, but restlessly expansionist, and the English who came to Ireland were not seeking converts. They were looking for personal gain, and just as they

The Butlers were among the
most powerful Anglo-Norman
families in Ireland, but the
figures decorating this early
sixteenth-century tomb of Piers
Og Butler at Kilcooly Abbey,
Co. Tipperary, wear Gaelic
dress and were carved by the
Irish stone carver Rory
O'Tunney.
Right: 'Black Tom' Butler, the
loyalist earl of Ormond,
decorated his late sixteenth-
century mansion at Carrick-on-
Suir, Co. Tipperary, with
plaster busts of Elizabeth I.

had no more respect for the Old English than they had for the native Irish, so also they showed little inclination to look with favour on those few of the other colonists who had become Protestant. There was no convincing evidence that conversion brought advantage and, in the event, far from following the English example, the Old English reacted against the uncongenial ethos of England and turned to the continent for their education. There they encountered the invigorated and modernised Catholicism of the Counter-Reformation and their acceptance of it set them sharply apart from the still traditionally inclined native Irish, though officialdom was slow to understand the significance of that division. Officials presumed that Catholic birds of a feather would flock together. But the Old English remained, like their predecessors, a 'middle nation', repudiated by their fellow Englishmen, repudiating their Irish fellow Catholics.

It was an impossible position to sustain for long. In the words of Cecil Day Lewis, 'only ghosts can live between two fires', and when the Ulster Irish rose in rebellion in 1641, the Old English saw no alternative but to join them in self-protection against the greed of the new settlers and the militant Protestantism of the English parliament and its Scottish allies. The outcome of the war which followed, and of the English Civil War which was fought alongside it, determined the fate of the old colony. The defeat of the Confederate Catholics, as the Old English and the Irish called themselves – more hopefully than accurately – and the triumph of Cromwell and the English parliamentary armies, formed a bizarre epilogue to the long-drawn-out conquest of Ireland as the descendants of the original conquerors were themselves conquered in their turn. In the aftermath, the Cromwellian land settlement, only slightly modified at the Restoration of Charles II in 1660, and the Williamite confiscations of the 1690s achieved the degradation of the Old English. Their inherited lands were lost and their descendants tumbled down the social scale to be submerged in the peasantry and become what they had never wished to be, Irish to both English and Irish alike.

There were some who escaped that fate. The history of individual families is not necessarily the same as that of the group as a whole. Although the lines of division between the Old and New English were firmly drawn, they were not impassable. In the seventeenth century, conversion to Protestantism might well suffice to convert an Old Englishman into a New Englishman. The king's chief representative in Ireland, both during the wars of the 1640s and after the Restoration – James Butler, duke of Ormond – was of Old English stock, and many of those he fought against were his close relatives. Less well known is the significant degree of movement which took place in the opposite direction, as a sizeable minority of the descendants of post-Reformation settlers became assimilated, adopted Catholicism, and, in the long run, paid the penalty. The classic case is that of Edmund Spenser – poet, Munster planter, and leading ideologue of the Tudor conquest of Ireland – whose immediate descendants lost their lands as 'Irish papists' in the 1650s. That was not an unusual outcome. In the midlands, particularly, post-plantation developments saw many families dividing as the junior branches, stemming from poorly endowed younger sons, went native. In the 1640s, there were many settler cousins in arms against one another. The principles of group association were cultural in character, and choice did exist. Thus it was that not all members of the Old English group shared in the downfall of their fellows. A prominent few managed to make the adaptations necessary to survival, to renounce their historic identity, and to conform to the new ethos.

After 1660, colonial Ireland was Protestant Ireland. A new colony, more representative of what England had become, had replaced the old one. In time, it too was to discover the predicaments of colonial status and face the difficulties of maintaining a satisfactory relationship with a mother country that went on changing. Like their predecessors, these colonists seemed English to the Irish and Irish to the English; perhaps this was because they were, as their predecessors had been, and as Maurice Fitzgerald had not foreseen, both Irish and English.

8

The Anglo-Irish

The influence of the Anglo-Irish in Ireland was at its height in the eighteenth century, and the institutions, edifices and outstanding literature which they bequeathed to modern Ireland are still important features of contemporary Irish life.

J. C. Beckett

I MUST start by asking a question: who are the Anglo-Irish? At first sight the answer must seem obvious: they are people of mixed English and Irish ancestry. But, in fact, this definition serves no useful purpose. England and Ireland have been closely associated for about eight hundred years, and during that period there has been so much intermarriage between English and Irish that at least half the population of Ireland – and probably a good deal more – must have some English element in their ancestry. We cannot, then, interpret 'Anglo-Irish' in this simple, straightforward way. We can only get at its meaning by asking how it is used.

It is, in fact, a term of fairly recent invention; and when it first became current it was applied, not to people, but to literature. At the end of the last century and the beginning of the present there was a group of Irish writers, who, though they wrote in English, tried to give their poems, plays and essays a distinctively Irish character. Their work was described by some contemporary critics as 'Anglo-Irish literature' – and later on, this term was extended backwards in time to include all writing in English by Irish-born authors.

During the past few generations, however, it has become the fashion to apply the term 'Anglo-Irish' to people as well as to literature. To begin with at least, the purpose was to imply that the people so described were not Irish at all – or, at best, a kind of second-class or mongrel Irish. Stephen Gwynn, the well-known

Irish author and politician, complained about this:

> I was brought up to think myself Irish without question or qual-
> ification, but the new nationalism prefers to describe me and
> the like of me as Anglo-Irish.

It is easy to understand Gwynn's complaint. His life was devoted
to Ireland. His best-known literary work is Irish in subject matter;
in politics he was a Nationalist – he represented Galway at
Westminster as a Home Rule M.P. from 1906 to 1918; and though
his father's family had settled in Ireland within the fairly recent
past, his mother was an O'Brien; and, through her, he could claim
to be descended from Brian Boru, the famous victor of the battle
of Clontarf in 1014. Gwynn might well feel that he had as much
right as anyone else to call himself Irish, without any qualifying
prefix.

Protests of this sort, however reasonable, had no effect; and the
term 'Anglo-Irish' is still used to describe one section of the population of Ireland – indeed, it seems to me that it has become more
common than it was a generation ago. But during this period it
has changed, if not in meaning, then in tone. It is used to describe
a recognisable section of the population; but the implication that
that section is, in some way, less truly Irish than the rest, is not
now so strongly marked as it was, though it may not have entirely
disappeared. And here I must add that in my view Gwynn was
right and that he and the like of him were – and are – as truly
Irish as any other inhabitant of the country.

I have just now spoken of the Anglo-Irish as 'a recognisable
section of the population'. But how is that section to be recognised? And so we come back to the question with which I began:
who are the Anglo-Irish? To get an answer we must go back to
the eighteenth century; for nowadays it is most commonly in
speaking or writing of the eighteenth century that the term is used.
That century was the century of what is commonly called 'the
Protestant Ascendancy'; when we speak of the 'Anglo-Irish' we
mean the people to whom that ascendancy belonged. And who
were they? They were the members of the established church, the
Church of Ireland. In Irish usage of the eighteenth century – and,
indeed, until much later – a Protestant meant a member of the
established church, as distinct from a Roman Catholic on the one
hand or a Presbyterian on the other. So what we may for convenience call 'Anglo-Irishness' is not so much a matter of ancestry as

a matter of culture, in the broad sense of the term. The Anglo-Irish were – and, so far as they survive, still are – those connected (though it may be by birth rather than conviction) with the Church of Ireland. If you were to read over a list of the men who took a leading part in re-organising the church after its disestablishment in 1869 it would sound very much like a roll-call of the Irish parliament in the eighteenth century.

So much by way of definition; and now we must try to assess the contribution of the Anglo-Irish to the life of their country. In doing so, it is natural to concentrate on the eighteenth century, when their influence was at its height. It is by what they did then that their achievement must be judged – and in passing judgement we must remember that we cannot fairly apply the standards of the present day to the conduct of people who lived two hundred years ago.

In considering the character and achievement of the Anglo-Irish of the eighteenth century we must first of all get rid of a common, but mistaken, idea that they consisted of no more than a small group of landlord families. The Anglo-Irish as I have defined them formed a substantial body – somewhere between a fifth and a sixth of the whole population. As was natural at that period the landlords and their families were politically and socially dominant. But they did not form a closed group. People could and did move up the social ladder. I take two striking examples. First, William Conolly – whose name, by the way, reminds us that the Anglo-Irish included families of Gaelic origin. Now Conolly's background was so obscure that the date of his birth is unknown; and it is a matter of doubt whether his father was a blacksmith or a publican. But, somehow or other, he pushed his way upwards; and when he died, in 1729, he had acquired a landed estate, he was Speaker of the House of Commons, and he was reputed to be one of the wealthiest men in the country. Next, Patrick Delany: his father started life as a domestic servant and later became tenant of a small farm. But Patrick managed to get a college education; he became a close friend of Swift; and in his later life he was one of the leading figures in the fashionable society of Dublin. Not many people – either in Ireland or elsewhere at that period – climbed so high from such humble beginnings; but these examples remind us that the aristocratic society of eighteenth-century Ireland was not – like the society of France at that period – a closed society, confined to people of aristocratic birth. A dramatic rise from poverty to riches was unusual – as, indeed, it still is; but, so far as the Protestant population was concerned, there were no impassable barriers. There was a fairly steady succession of well-to-do merchants who purchased landed property and thus made their way into the ruling class; for it was, as in England at the same period, the landlords who dominated both houses of parliament.

It is not, however, about the political life of the Anglo-Irish that I am concerned here. The issues they debated in parliament, the bills they supported or opposed, belong to the past. I prefer to judge them by what has survived to the present. And I start with two surviving memorials of their concern for the welfare of their country – the Dublin Society (now the Royal Dublin Society), founded in 1731, and the Royal Irish Academy, which received its charter in 1786.

The man who took the lead in founding the Dublin Society was Thomas Prior, a well-to-do landlord. Like Swift, he was much concerned about the poverty he found in many parts of the country; but, unlike Swift, he was not content to complain and scold – he was resolved to do something to improve the situation. It was for this purpose that he, along with some of his friends, established the Dublin Society. Its purpose was to improve the standard of agriculture, both by precept and by example; to encourage manufactures; and to provide training in what at that period were called 'the useful arts' – and for Prior these arts included both architecture and painting. All this cost a good deal of money; and Prior and his friends could have done little without generous public support. From 1749 onwards the society received a parliamentary grant of £500 a year; but this covered only a fraction of its outlay; and it still had to depend heavily upon voluntary subscriptions. A glance at the kind of people who did subscribe gives us a fair idea of the make-up of the well-to-do section of Anglo-Irish society: landlords, clergy, lawyers, merchants, shop-keepers. And it is only fair to Prior and his supporters to remember that in setting up and financing this society they were not following any example – they were setting one, for the Dublin Society was among the first of its kind in Europe. Nowadays, of course, most of the work that the society undertook is regarded as the business of government; and it is likely that at the present day the Royal Dublin Society (to give its later title) is best known for

Dunluce Castle, spectacularly situated on the north Antrim coast, was built by Richard de Burgh, earl of Ulster, around 1300 and taken by the McDonalds of the Isles in the sixteenth century. Their most prominent chieftain, Sorley Boy MacDonnell, was active in the struggle against English rule and his son James offered a safe haven to Spanish sailors shipwrecked on the Ulster coast after the defeat of the Spanish Armada in 1588. *Overleaf: Battle of Ballynahinch, Co. Down, 13 June, 1798* by Thomas Robinson. The tragedy of 1798 was that what the United Irishmen intended to be a crusade for Irish liberty and against injustice became a civil war. If descendants of Scots settlers fought as rebels in counties Antrim and Down, they were also prominent in the ranks of the yeomanry in Fermanagh, Tyrone, Derry and Armagh.

Top: A French visitor described late eighteenth-century Belfast as having 'completely the look of a Scotch town and the character of its inhabitants shows considerable resemblance to the people of Glasgow'.

Above: The Royal Belfast Academical Institution, in the centre of Belfast, was founded in 1810 to offer educational standards to the sons of Ulster Scots not too far removed from those of an English public school. Today its pupils come from many backgrounds.

Tired after a day in the field: William of Orange enjoys the steadfast support of Ulstermen of all ages, three hundred years after the Battle of the Boyne.

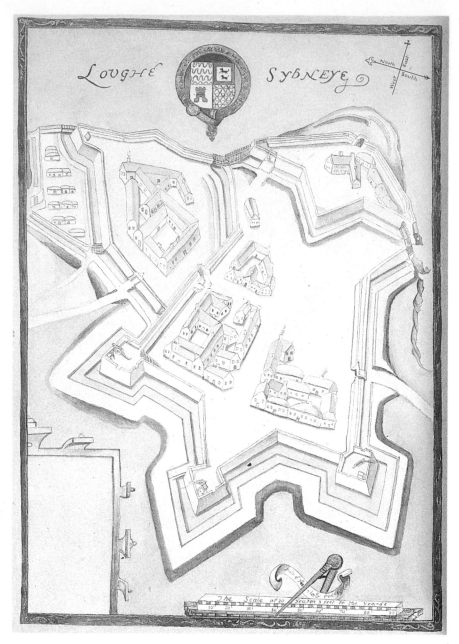

The defeat of Hugh O'Neill, earl of Tyrone, dramatically expanded English settlement in Ireland. This early map (1602) of Mountjoy Fort in the heartland of O'Neill territory shows a town already growing up within the walls. In the top left an 'Irishtown' of thatched huts can be seen, segregated from the rest as in older cities like Limerick and Galway.

Opposite: An English portrait of Elizabeth Fitzgerald (the 'Fair Geraldine'), daughter of Garret Og, earl of Kildare. This painting, from the first half of the sixteenth century, is the earliest known formal portrait of an Irish person.

Jonathan Swift (1667-1745), Dean of St Patrick's Cathedral, Dublin and the first of the great Anglo-Irish writers. Swift's Gulliver found Lilliput in a constant state of civil war between those who opened their boiled eggs at the thin end and those who opened them at the thick.

Left: Most of Dublin's great public buildings are products of the Anglo-Irish Ascendancy. Thomas Gandon's Four Courts was built between 1786 and 1802. In 1922 it withstood three days of almost continuous shelling during the Civil War. The adjoining Public Record Office was less fortunate: it was destroyed, along with the priceless historical archives it contained.

137

The Vere-Foster Family by Orpen. Not all of the Anglo-Irish were wealthy country gentlemen, yet hunting, shooting and fishing were central to their way of life, lending some substance to Brendan Behan's definition of an Anglo-Irishman as a Protestant on a horse.

Baronscourt in Co. Tyrone *(opposite, above)*, the seat of the Dukes of Abercorn. The heart of rural Anglo-Irish aristocratic life was the big house, with its gardens and parkland.

Within their doors, some of the great Georgian mansions attained a quality of decoration and furnishing not equalled in Ireland before. Castletown House, Co. Kildare *(opposite, below)*, has recently been restored to its former glory by the Georgian society.

139

The Itinerant Preacher by Nathaniel Grogan. The travelling Wesleyan
preacher was a common enough sight in eighteenth-century Ireland for
Grogan to use it as a subject for this painting of contemporary Irish social
life.

Opposite: Ireland has assimilated many religious faiths. Christian symbols at
a Holy Well in Co. Clare represent traditional religious practice, while at
nearby Lisdoonvarna a member of the Krishna Consciousness Movement
explains his beliefs at a local music festival.

Overleaf: Night's Candles are Burnt Out. Sean Keating's allegorical painting
depicts some of the stereotypical figures of post-Independence Irish society.

KEATING.

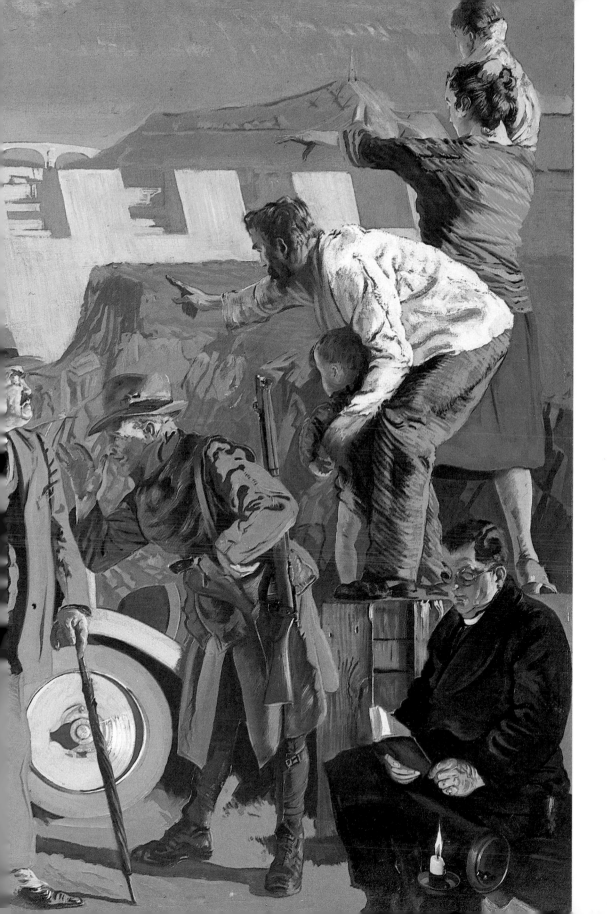

A tribe within a tribe, the travelling people are an alienated minority in Irish society, the victims of greater discrimination than ethnic groups like the Indians or Chinese.

its annual horse show. But Prior and his friends had a much more serious purpose than to improve the breed of horses and to provide a gala day for the middle and upper classes.

The Dublin Society was set up to do something that had rarely been attempted before, anywhere in Europe. The other great institution inherited from the eighteenth-century Anglo-Irish – the Royal Irish Academy – follows a well-established pattern. There were similar bodies in many parts of Europe; but it was modelled mainly on the Royal Society in England, which had been founded in the reign of Charles II. This resolve to have a distinctively Irish body devoted to the encouragement of what was then commonly called 'polite learning' reflects what we might term the 'cultural' nationalism of the Anglo-Irish; and the Academy, though it has not neglected other fields of study, has alway encouraged scholarly work of Irish interest – as, for example, in language, literature, archaeology and history.

The Royal Dublin Society and the Royal Irish Academy may be regarded as part of the living legacy of the eighteenth-century Anglo-Irish. But they have left also a legacy in stone – their architecture. This brings me back to Speaker Conolly – but not to his career as a politician. There must be many hundreds, perhaps thousands, of people who know nothing about his reputation as Speaker of the House of Commons, who, indeed, may never have heard his name, but who have seen and admired his most lasting achievement – his house, Castletown, in Co. Kildare, which is one of the most splendid examples of Georgian architecture in Ireland. And we must remember that Conolly did not simply order the house to be built and then pay the architect and the builder. Indeed, there is some doubt as to who the architect was; but we know that Conolly himself took an active part in designing the house and that he, along with a group of his friends, supervised its construction. The finished product is a monument to his taste as well as to his wealth.

Castletown is not an isolated example of the good taste shown by the eighteenth-century Anglo-Irish. Throughout Ireland there are hundreds of Georgian houses – some large, some small, some very simple in design, some more elaborate. But all are marked by a sureness of taste that seems strangely out of keeping with the popular reputation of the men for whom they were built. The traditional picture of the eighteenth-century Irish squire portrays him as a reckless spendthrift, with little interest in anything but hunting, drinking and duelling. Such characters no doubt existed – they were to be found among the landed class of every country in Europe; but it is only in works of fiction that they are typical of the Irish gentry as a whole.

These country houses are not the only architectural legacy that the Anglo-Irish have left to succeeding generations. Dublin, as we know it today, is very largely their creation. Down to the end of the seventeenth century Dublin had little to boast of in the way of great buildings, apart from the two cathedrals inherited from the middle ages. The castle was, in the words of a lord deputy of Charles II's time, 'the worst castle on the worst site in Christendom'; but it was during Charles's reign that the transformation of Dublin into the city we know today had its beginnings. The change was inaugurated by James Butler, twelfth earl and first duke of Ormond. Ormond, the first of the Butlers to be brought up as a Protestant, died in 1688; but he might fairly be regarded as a prototype of the Anglo-Irish of the following century, and not least in his care for the proper development of Dublin. It was he, for example, who saved the Phoenix Park for the city – but for him, Charles II would have given it as a present to one of his numerous mistresses.

Ormond's contribution to the development of Dublin was mainly preparatory. The only important building that belongs to his time is the Royal Hospital at Kilmainham. But this set an example of good taste that was followed in the architecture of the eighteenth century, not only in the great public buildings – the Parliament House, the Four Courts, the Custom House – but also in the streets and squares where the wealthier citizens lived and where the nobility and gentry had their town houses. And it is this domestic architecture, quite as much as the great public buildings, that gives Dublin its distinctive character.

The architectural legacy of the eighteenth century belongs, by its nature, to Ireland. The literary legacy of the period belongs to the whole English-speaking world. There is another difference also. The country houses and the great public buildings were built at the expense of, or under the direction of, the ruling class – the nobility and gentry. But when we turn from architecture to literature we move to a different social level. All the great Anglo-Irish writers of the period, and most of the minor ones as well, belong to the middle ranks of society. If we take both major and minor writers together the number of those who attained some reputation in their own day and whose names still survive – at least in the histories of literature – we must say that the Anglo-Irish produced, in relation to their numbers, a very large crop of authors. But their high literary reputation depends essentially upon the work of five men – Swift, Berkeley, Goldsmith, Sheridan and Burke. It is worth noting that these five represent between them four different strains in the Anglo-Irish population. Swift and Berkeley were born and educated in Ireland; but their parents were recent arrivals from England. Goldsmith's family had been settled in Ireland for some generations. Burke was descended, on both sides of his family, from Anglo-Norman settlers of the medieval period. Sheridan was a Gael – his ancestors had dropped the O from before their name in the seventeenth century, perhaps at the same time as they became Protestant. It is interesting to note that of these five the one whose reputation stands highest in Ireland is Swift, the newcomer; and that Sheridan, the Gael, is the one in whose work the Irish influence seems weakest.

This list of names is, by itself, enough to indicate how great was the literary achievement of the eighteenth-century Anglo-Irish, for it would be hard to find five English-born writers of the period whose work surpasses – or, indeed, even equals – that of the men I have named. There is no space here to discuss their work in detail. But I would draw attention to one significant aspect of their achievement; throughout the eighteenth century the theatre was very popular, both in Ireland and in England, and new plays were constantly being written. But of all those written during the last three-quarters of the century the only ones that survive as literature – or, indeed, upon the stage – are those of Goldsmith and Sheridan. When we add to this the fact that among the dramatists of the period whose plays are now almost or quite forgotten there was a surprisingly large proportion of Irishmen, we are almost forced to the conclusion that there is something in the Anglo-Irish character or experience that is particularly favourable to the drama. This seems to be borne out by their achievement at a later period – I may mention, for example, Oscar Wilde, Bernard Shaw and Denis Johnson.

I said earlier that the literary legacy of the Anglo-Irish belongs to the whole English-speaking world. But they also contributed something essentially Irish. Among the minor playwrights and novelists of the period was Henry Brooke. There was nothing Irish about his play or his novel; but in later life he became interested in Irish history and legend. He even began to write – though he never completed – a long narrative poem based on the legendary history of ancient Ulster. What is much more important is that his example encouraged his daughter, Charlotte Brooke, to take an interest in Gaelic. She learned the language and set about collecting and translating songs and poems traditional among the Gaelic peasantry. She was not, of course , alone in her interest in Gaelic literature. Joseph Cooper Walker, a Dublin antiquary, published his *Historical memoirs of the Irish bards* in 1786; and it was he who encouraged Charlotte Brooke to publish her translations. Her book, *Reliques of Irish poetry*, which contained both the original text and her own verse translations, was published in Dublin in 1789. Here we have the first glimmer of the 'Gaelic Revival' of the next century, in which the Anglo-Irish were to play a very important part.

The year that saw the publication of *Reliques of Irish poetry* saw also the outbreak of the French Revolution; and Ireland, like the rest of Europe, felt its effect. Some years earlier, Edmund Burke, speaking of the relationship between Ireland and England, had said that he did not see any need for a parliamentary union between the two, save (to use his own words) 'in some nearly desperate crisis of the empire'. One effect of the French Revolution was to produce just such a crisis, though not until ten years after its outbreak. In Ireland, as elsewhere in Europe, there were those who welcomed the revolution and wished to apply its principles in their own country. It was they who established the Society of United Irishmen, with the aim of remodelling the government and society of Ireland after the pattern of republican France; and when they rose in insurrection in 1798 it was with the expectation that the French would send forces to assist them. But French help, when it came, was too little and too late; and the insurrection was suppressed. The rank and file of the insurgent forces consisted, for the most part, of Roman Catholics and Presbyterians; but among the leaders of the movement that led to the insurrection the two who are most widely remembered were both Anglo-Irish: Lord Edward FitzGerald and Wolfe Tone – the one an aristocrat, the other a member of a typical middle-class family.

There is something in the Anglo-Irish character or experience that is particularly favourable to the drama. George Bernard Shaw (1856-1950) is one of the best known of the many Anglo-Irish playwrights.

Burke had died the year before the insurrection broke out; but it had produced just the kind of crisis he had described and it was quickly followed by the remedy he had proposed – a parliamentary union between Ireland and Great Britain. The ruling class among the Anglo-Irish had, quite naturally, been alarmed by the insurrection. But once it was crushed they recovered their self-confidence; and they were very unwilling to allow their parliament to be abolished. This feeling was so strong that the government did not dare to test public opinion by holding a general election; and it was only after long debates and a lavish use of bribery, in one form or another, that the Act of Union was at length passed. But when the act had been passed even those who had opposed it to the end – Grattan, for example – came to accept it as something final and enduring. Within a generation the maintenance of the union had become, for the great majority of the Anglo-Irish, the basic principle of their politics. Those of them who wished to see it modified or repealed (though they included some men of outstanding ability) were never more than a tiny minority of the whole body.

It is unlikely that any of the Anglo-Irish, whether they had opposed the union or supported it, could have foreseen the fundamental change that it would make in their own position. From this time onwards they had no means of taking any collective action; and such political influence as they retained after the union steadily declined, as successive reforms of parliament enlarged the electorate. Their fate now depended upon others rather than upon themselves. Within a relatively short time most of them came to regard the union with Great Britain as essential to their security – they were convinced that, whatever they might suffer in the way of loss of influence under the parliament at Westminster, they would lose a great deal more under a parliament in Dublin: for, as a result of changes made since the union, that parliament would now be sure to contain a majority of Roman Catholics. O'Connell, when he was campaigning for the repeal of the Act of Union, had endeavoured to reassure the Protestants; but he himself had done a good deal, however unintentionally, to create the impression that the Irish nation was identical with the Catholic population. His newspaper, the *Pilot*, put it quite bluntly: the 'positive and unmistakable' mark of distinction between Irish and English was, it declared, 'the distinction created by religion'.

Though the bulk of the Anglo-Irish, once they had accepted the Union, stood by it to the end, there were in every generation some who supported the cause of Irish Nationalism. One such was Charles Stewart Parnell, the ultimately tragic leader of the campaign for Home Rule for Ireland.

But though the bulk of the Anglo-Irish, once they had accepted the union, stood by it to the end, there were, in every generation, some of them who supported the cause of Irish nationalism – Thomas Davis, William Smith O'Brien (grandfather of Stephen Gwynn), Charles Stewart Parnell, to name only three of the most famous. But these, and others who took the same stand, had no following among the rank and file of the Anglo-Irish, who were convinced that their security, if not their survival, depended upon the maintenance of the union.

Their steady support for the union must not be taken to mean that they ceased to regard themselves as Irish; and whatever may be said of their political views, they themselves believed that the policy they advocated was best, not just for themselves, but for their country. In some respects they were more self-consciously Irish than their eighteenth-century predecessors. The Anglo-Irish writers of that period had rarely written on Irish themes except when they were concerned with political or economic or social questions. Their successors in the nineteenth and twentieth centuries found in Irish life, past and present, material for imaginative literature – novels, poems, plays.

It was, in fact, in 1801, the year when the union came into force, that the first novel of Irish life appeared – Maria Edgeworth's *Castle Rackrent*. This example, it should be remembered, inspired Walter Scott to write a novel of Scottish life, though *Waverley* was not published until fourteen years later. Miss Edgeworth's example was followed more quickly in Ireland. Lady Morgan's *Wild Irish Girl* appeared in 1806; and from then until the present day there has been a steady succession of Irish novelists. Not all of them, of course, belong to the Anglo-Irish tradition; but those who do include some of the best known: Samuel Lover, Charles Lever, Somerville and Ross.

But the most characteristic expression of what we might call 'literary nationalism' among the Anglo-Irish of the nineteenth century was not the novel, but a periodical, *The Dublin University Magazine*, which first appeared in 1833 and remained for more than forty years the most important literary periodical published in Ireland. Not all its contributors belonged to the Anglo-Irish community – William Carleton, for example, published much of his later work there before it appeared in book form. But the men who founded the magazine, the policy it followed and the public on whose support it depended were all characteristically Anglo-Irish.

The three original directors of the Abbey Theatre, William Butler Yeats (1865-1939) (*left*), Lady Gregory (1852-1932) and John Millington Synge (1871-1909). Yeats tried to create a literature which, though English in language, would be Irish in character.

Among the contributors to the *Dublin University Magazine* there was one whose influence was of outstanding importance – more important, indeed, than his own writings. This was Sir Samuel Ferguson who, despite his Scottish ancestry, clearly belongs to the cultural tradition of the Anglo-Irish. Ferguson set himself to make the legendary history of ancient Ireland familiar to his own generation, both by his translations from the Gaelic and by poems and stories based on Gaelic legend and history. Ferguson never reached a large public, and today it is probable that not many people read either his prose or his verse – except, perhaps, for the few of his poems that still appear in anthologies. What makes him so important is the influence he had on Yeats, who described him as 'the greatest poet that Ireland has produced'.

Yeats certainly overrated Ferguson's poetry. But we must remember that at the time he paid this tribute to Ferguson he, with others, was trying to create a literature that, though English in language, should be Irish in character. One means by which they hoped to accomplish this was by the use of Gaelic legend and mythology. It is significant that not only Yeats himself but also the five others most closely associated with him were all Anglo-Irish. And three of them – Yeats himself, Lady Gregory and J. M. Synge – were the original directors of the Abbey Theatre, which may fairly be regarded as a distinctively Anglo-Irish creation.

More than eighty years have now passed since the opening of the Abbey Theatre; and during that period the influence of the Anglo-Irish has steadily declined. Some would say, indeed, that it has already gone; and that the Anglo-Irish, in so far as they survive at all count for nothing in the life of their country. This may be so. But of two things I am sure: the Anglo-Irish have a past to be proud of; and Ireland without them will be a poorer place.

9

Religious Minorities

Irish Protestantism often bears the appearance of a parochial monolith but it has, in fact, engagingly diverse and internationalist elements within it: Methodists, Huguenots, Palatines, Moravians and Quakers have all made their mark on the wider Irish culture.

David Hempton

POST-REFORMATION Europe was not a happy place for religious minorities, Protestant or Catholic. The dynastic rivalries and insecurities of late medieval Europe were made more acute by the Protestant Reformation and the Catholic Counter-Reformation. With toleration unthinkable, most states responded with severe measures against religious deviants who were thought to be both socially undesirable and politically unsafe. The severity of religious persecution depended in the first instance upon the seriousness of the perceived threat, but it was always intensified by foreign wars or domestic instability. Such conditions were the rule, not the exception, in sixteenth and seventeenth-century Europe. The most characteristic consequence of state repression and international warfare, then as now, was the creation of large numbers of displaced persons. Indeed the very word 'refugee', with which sadly we are now all too familiar, was first used of those seventeenth-century French Calvinists, or Huguenots, who fled from the intolerance of successive French monarchs, especially Louis XIV.

Of the myriads of Protestant refugees who made their way across Europe and even into the New World in the early modern period, representatives of two groups, the Huguenots and the Palatines, found their way to Ireland. Huguenots were not new to Ireland in the late seventeenth century, but the most important wave of settlers (about 10,000) came in the wake of the Revocation in 1685 of the toleration offered by the Edict of Nantes. France's loss was Ireland's gain, for Huguenots brought with them military expertise, liquid capital, trading networks and a range of skills from linen manufacturing to sail-making. In particular they made a telling, if often exaggerated, contribution to William of Orange's Irish campaigns and to the development of the linen industry. Moreover, Huguenot descendants played a significant role in the development of Irish commerce and banking, literature and architecture, map-making and surveying; but in the well-known lists of contributors and contributions it is sometimes forgotten that the real reason for Huguenot migration was to obtain freedom of worship. Here too they were successful, but at a price.

Huguenots were welcomed by the Protestant Ascendancy in early eighteenth-century Ireland for their industry and their Protestantism. Conformity to the Church of Ireland was made profitable, nonconformity relatively easy, and access to the social elite was kept open. As a result the Huguenots, despite sharing a common language, culture and theology, were slowly assimilated into a wider Irish Protestantism. Widely practised intermarriage and controlled apprenticeships merely slowed down the pace of assimilation without affecting its eventual outcome.

Ironically perhaps, far more Huguenot descendants entered the hierarchy of the Church of Ireland than ever joined the ranks of those other Calvinistic settlers, the Ulster-Scots Presbyterians. Not all Huguenot congregations conformed to the Church of Ireland however, and those that did were allowed to retain some elements of their French Presbyterian past. Nevertheless, Irish Huguenots, in common with other Huguenot communities in Western Europe, were either unwilling or unable to sustain a distinctively French culture beyond the third or fourth generation. The last of the French churches closed their doors in the early nineteenth century. Only the graveyards remained as the last gesture of the unassimilated. What remains of the Huguenot presence in Ireland cannot be adequately assessed in terms of the architectural curiosities of Portarlington or the survival of French surnames. Its real contribution was to add, in however limited a degree, a certain dynamism to Irish society and through that to enrich its host civilisation. Small minorities cannot be expected to do much more.

An even smaller minority, equally the victim of the Sun King's

Weaver Samuel Dupré, a descendant of Mark Henry Dupré, the Huguenot reedmaker who settled in Lisburn, Co. Antrim, in the late seventeenth century. *Left*: Quakers provided soup kitchens to feed the starving during the potato famine of the late 1840s.

brutality, was the German Palatine community which arrived in Ireland in 1709. After suffering successive devastations of the Palatinate through war and economic distress, 821 families arrived in Dublin via London and were settled in estates in Limerick, Kerry and Tipperary. These humble German farmers were given land under decidedly favourable terms, much to the chagrin of their native Irish neighbours. To a greater degree than other religious and ethnic minorities in Ireland the Palatines lived as a distinct people separated from the indigenous population by language, culture, religion, folk memories, farming methods and relative prosperity. Aided by their general rural seclusion and fervent Protestantism, which was later rekindled by John Wesley and the Methodists, the Palatines resisted assimilation by practising strict intermarriage and by regulating their own affairs through an appointed burgomaster. Even when their native language disappeared around 1800 and they experienced greater economic integration in the post-Famine period, the Palatines still retained subtle elements of their late nineteenth-century Germanic origins until well into the twentieth century.

There is one important postscript to the Palatine settlements in Ireland, for the majority of settlers left after their favourable leases ran out in 1760. Some Palatine migrants, having encountered Methodism in Ireland, moved on to North America where they founded the first Methodist churches in the American colonies, and later, as Empire loyalists, in Canada as well. Indeed, the Great Awakening, or Evangelical Revival, of the eighteenth century – so often studied within absurdly narrow geographical boundaries – was largely borne on the wings of the recurrent folk migrations of displaced Protestant minorities as they made their way across Europe and into the New World. Ireland, as Europe's last off-shore island, and as an unrivalled exporter of humanity, played a strategic role in such migrations.

If Palatine migrants from Ireland made an important contribution to religious life in North America, an encounter between John Wesley and another German pietist community, the Moravians, on a ship bound for America was to have profound ramifications for religious life in Ireland. Wesley, after his Moravian-inspired 'conversion' in 1738, looked upon the world – even Ireland – as his parish, and he made twenty-one preaching visits there between 1747 and 1789. Wesley professed a genuine love for the

Irish, but they did not always love him or his travelling band of itinerant preachers, disparagingly nicknamed Black Caps, Swaddlers and 'cavalry preachers'. The old Methodist class ticket motto 'Everywhere spoken against' was particularly appropriate in Ireland, where unsympathetic authorities – civil, ecclesiastical and legal – abandoned early Methodists to the licence of the crowd. Licence became mayhem in Cork between 1749 and 1751 when Nicholas Butler, an eccentric ballad-singer, mock preacher and rabble rouser, led the city mobs in repeated anti-Methodist forays. It was the most sustained outbreak of anti-Methodist rioting in eighteenth-century Britain or Ireland. Fortunately for the Methodists such intense opposition proved transitory, and by the end of the eighteenth century Methodist expansion was relatively unchecked by popular hostility.

When Wesley died in 1791 there were about 15,000 Irish men and women enrolled in Methodist societies with twice as many again coming under the influence of Methodist preaching. Before 1770 such growth had taken place mainly in southern Irish cities and market towns. But increasingly from the 1780s, Methodism grew most rapidly within the traditionally Anglican populations of the Fermanagh lakelands and the 'linen triangle' of south Ulster. Such growth reached revivalist proportions in the aftermath of the rebellion of the United Irishmen in 1798. In these dark years Gaelic-speaking Methodist missionaries, to use their own words, 'denounced the judgements of heaven against the crimes of a guilty nation'. So successful was Methodist recruitment in the province of Ulster in the turbulent years at the turn of the century that by 1815 two-thirds of Irish Methodists lived north of a line drawn from Sligo to Dundalk, whereas half a century earlier two-thirds lived south of that line. As recent demographic surveys have brought to light, the concentration of Protestantism in the northern part of Ireland is a feature not only of Presbyterian history, but is of much wider application in pre-Famine Ireland.

Early Methodism in Ireland threw up a host of engaging characters, from Gideon Ouseley, a Gaelic-speaking evangelist who at his peak travelled 4,000 miles a year and preached twenty times a week, to Lorenzo Dow – or Crazy Dow as he was unkindly known – an asthmatic Kentucky frontier preacher who was the first in a long line of American revivalists to visit Ireland. Of more modern relevance perhaps, eighteenth-century Methodism made occasional use of female preachers and experimented with various forms of charity including imitation of the early church's sharing of goods.

What then did Methodism, as the largest religious minority in Ireland in the period 1750-1900, contribute to the society in which it developed? First, it introduced into Ireland a new kind of associational, voluntaristic and non-credal religion which has its roots in seventeenth-century continental pietism. Wesley's 'religion of the heart' and commitment to holy charity, descibed by one theologian as a sort of evangelical Catholicism, was an attempt to move away from the ecclesiastical polarisation which had afflicted European society in the post-Reformation period. His network of religious societies, serviced by itinerant preachers and committed to the spiritual disciplines of self-examination, worship, fellowship and education, brought a new dimension to the Irish religious landscape, which until then had been dominated by churches ministering to pre-assigned communities. Although early Methodists were far more concerned with 'saving the lost' than in poaching from other churches, their conversionist message inevitably introduced a new competitiveness to Irish religion. It is, however, one of the paradoxes of Irish history that early Methodist missionaries, by preaching in Irish, were better conservators of Gaelic culture than the more europeanised section of the Catholic priesthood.

Perhaps Methodism's most important contribution to Irish society was the stimulus it gave to a much wider evangelicalism, initially in the Dublin area and then in the province of Ulster in the nineteenth century. Many Methodist characteristics, particularly itinerant preaching and the idea of non-institutional voluntary religious societies, were taken up by individuals, missionary organisations and eventually by the churches themselves. To begin with at least, this upsurge in 'serious religion' transcended the old ecclesiastical boundaries and resuscitated those slumbering survivors from Cromwellian times, the Anabaptists and the Independents, or as they were then known, the Baptists and the Congregationalists.

With a faith nurtured in rural Ulster in the period 1790-1820, evangelicals of all denominations then worked for the redemption of Belfast's rapidly increasing industrial population. Through the activities of Sunday schools, Bible and tract societies, city missions, sabbatarian and temperance movements, home mission and domestic visitation societies, and organisations unlimited for the reformation of vice and the promotion of virtue, literally tens of thousands of Belfast people committed themselves to systematic religious benevolence of one kind or another. Here was a sub-culture the sheer activism of which made it the dominant ethos of popular Protestantism in Belfast and Ulster in the Victorian era. To admit that many of the labouring classes remained untouched by its reforming clutches, and that some of its benevolence was narrow, crude and partisan, is not to diminish the power of this culture nor its intrinsic value for many humble people whose lives were shaped by the weekly rhythms of religious preparation and activity. No history of the northern part of Ireland can be written without paying due attention to its mores.

Finally, it would be wrong to leave Methodism without paying some tribute to its contribution to Sunday, elementary and secondary education in Ireland as a whole and to its remarkable participation in world mission in the period after 1760. There were not many parts of the world unvisited by an Irish Methodist by 1900, though inevitably some native preoccupations were exported in the process.

If Wesley was the chief outside contributor to evangelical enthusiasm in eighteenth-century Ireland, he was not the only one. John Cennick, a Wiltshire itinerant preacher of Bohemian descent, arrived in Dublin in 1746 and quickly built up a large religious society in an old Baptist meeting house in Skinner's Alley. Cennick, as with many of the early evangelicals, had come under the influence of the Moravians – that is, the followers of the Ancient Church of the Brethren in Moravia, Bohemia and Poland. This church was reconstituted in the 1720s at Herrnhut (in present day East Germany) by the remarkable Count Zinzendorf. Herrnhut became the parent religious community of the Moravians who went on to establish religious settlements in central Europe, at Zeist in the Netherlands, Fulneck in Yorkshire, Bethlehem in Pennsylvania and, of course, Gracehill in Co. Antrim. The Gracehill community arose out of Cennick's prodigious, and all but forgotten, itinerant labours in Ulster in the period 1748-55, and was built after the Herrnhut model with Dutch and German help.

The aim was to establish a self-regulating Christian village with

John Wesley (1703–91)
preaching in Ireland.
Between 1747 and 1789
Wesley made twenty-one
visits to Ireland.
Left: The Moravian Church
at Gracehill, Co. Antrim.
This religious community
was founded with Dutch
and German help after the
English preacher John
Cennick had established the
faith in Ulster between 1748
and 1755.

a chapel, a school, an inn for travellers, and accommodation and workshops for single men and women. Indeed in early Moravian communities the separation of the sexes was enforced to the limit – at least until marriage. Another distinctive feature of the Moravians was that all community decisions were taken by drawing lots, however inconvenient the result.

The Moravian approach to evangelism envisaged the creation of numerous quasi-monastic settlements which would not only be inward-looking in the sense that the inhabitants would seek to live out a disciplined and charitable Christianity, but also outward-looking to work for the conversion of the world. To a remarkable extent for such a tiny religious minority, the Moravians spearheaded the international missionary movement, with missions as far apart as Greenland and South America, Labrador and South Africa. In Ireland, Gracehill for all its utopian idealism never attracted more than 500 to its community, and by 1850 non-Moravians were permitted to settle in its neat little squares.

It is impossible to walk around the Moravian settlements of Europe and not be moved by the stark simplicity of their pure white chapels with golden candlesticks and organ pipes, and the meticulously kept stone graveyards, with sexes still separate in death, awaiting the sure and certain hope that was to come. Ironically, much of this pietist beauty was financed by Zinzendorf, a display-oriented aristocrat of peacock proportions with a penchant for gambling and for playing the eighteenth-century version of the stock exchange until his luck finally ran out. Indeed, the links between pious businessmen and the international spread of popular Protestantism is one of the most intriguing stories in the history of the church.

The Moravians of Gracehill never fulfilled their high evangelistic aspirations in Ireland, though they achieved much else in the fields of education, fine craftsmanship and charity. But the Church of the United Brethren still survives as a living religious tradition in Ireland – a living witness to the power of the human spirit in those displaced Germanic minorities who shuffled across Europe to avoid persecution in the early modern world. The Moravians have also bequeathed to Ireland one of its most bizarre architectural curiosities in the shape of an earthwork model of the ancient classical battle at Thermopylae. This ancient Greek victory over the Persians was memorialised in Ireland by Basil

Patras Zula, an early nineteenth-century Greek refugee from the war of independence against Turkey. He was also the Moravian pastor of the little church of Kilwarlin near Moira.

It should be clear already that many of the ethnic and religious minorities in Ireland had their origins in the religious, social and dynastic upheavals caused by the Reformation and prolonged periods of European warfare. One of the most remarkable, in terms of its longevity, adaptability and social importance, is the Society of Friends — the Quakers — who had their origin in the many independent Puritan congregations which flourished in England in the aftermath of the English Civil Wars. Their founder, George Fox, was essentially a prophet and mystic who rejected artificial hierarchies and social distinctions — since the seed of God was in everyman — and consequently opposed oaths, tithes and church rates. They were established in Ireland in the early 1650s through the work of William Edmundson, an ex-Cromwellian soldier, who set up business in Lurgan before moving to Mountmellick.

Most of the early Quakers in Ireland were relatively poor migrants from northern England, but by 1850 they appear as an upper middle-class business community of few labourers and no gentry. As exponents of reinvestment rather than conspicuous consumption, the Irish Quakers made a profound contribution to every aspect of commercial life in modern Ireland including linen manufacturing, steamships, railways and foreign trade. Not all was success however; if not actively persecuted, Quakers were frequently imprisoned in the eighteenth century for refusal to pay tithes, and their declared neutrality was abused during the Williamite Wars and again during the rebellion of the United Irishmen. Their quaint ways often made them objects of ridicule but rarely of hatred, and by the mid-nineteenth century they were a much admired community throughout the British Isles.

Intensely conscious of their English identity, early Quakers practised strict intermarriage and refused to conform to the culture of the host population. Yet inexplicably, as their remarkably complete records show, Irish Quakers, despite sharing the same genetic stock and socio-economic characteristics as their English brethren, conformed more to pre-Famine Irish demographic patterns than to those of the English Quakers. To put it more crudely, living in Ireland enhanced Quaker fertility. This fact is not only suggestive of the complex forces that fuelled Ireland's rapid and ultimately tragic population explosion, but shows too that however unassimilated religious and ethnic minorities appear to be, host civilisations inevitably make their mark.

Quakerism in Ireland will be remembered most for its philanthropy and concern for social justice. By tapping the resources of American Friends, they made a still unrecorded contribution to famine relief quite disproportionate to their numbers, and were at the forefront of anti-slavery, temperance, prison reform, free trade and peace movements. Indeed, the sheer barbarity of world history in the twentieth century has made pacifism, which was once peripheral, one of Quakerism's central beliefs and, for some, its most essential element. By remaining suspicious of religious dogma and by retaining its humanitarian convictions, the Society of Friends has survived for three centuries from its unpromising roots in civil war sectarianism to make a distinctive contribution to strife-torn Ireland and the wider world.

This has been a rapid, and, inevitably, a highly selective tour through the landscape of Ireland's most colourful and influential minorities. More could have been said about a whole range of religious groups from the Plymouth Brethren to the modern pentecostal and charismatic renewal movements. Moreover, if Ireland in times gone by exported its religion to all corners of the globe, it has, since 1850, through Mormonism, Jehovah's Witnesses and even Hare Krishna received a new generation of religious minorities with their origins in North America and the East. Perhaps it should be left to the theologian, or even the sociologist, to work out the profit and the loss on this predominantly trans-Atlantic religious account. Such religious exchanges have given inhabitants of Belfast a wider range of religious choices than any other city of comparable size in Europe.

What conclusions then suggest themselves from this subject? First, there is a need for perspective. Religious minorities are precisely that, small groups of relatively powerless people drawn together by religious and/or ethnic identity. They never formed more than a tiny percentage of the total Irish population, and settled almost exclusively in the eastern part of the island and in seaports. But without capitulating to the exaggeration of some of their own histories, it is clear that they had an impact on Irish society and economy out of all proportion to their numbers. Moreover, it is tempting to account for the numerical weakness of religious minorities in Ireland by referring to the cultural dominance of more powerful Irish religions. But in truth the minorities who arrived in Ireland fared no worse than their co-religionists in other parts of Western Europe. Numbers were simply smaller in Ireland than elsewhere.

Secondly, as is true of all immigration, the pace and pattern of assimilation depended on a range of factors including social and geographical mobility, language, intermarriage, prosperity, religion, the strength of native resistance and the speed of social change. The Palatines, for example, assimilated slowly because they were distinctive in race, religion and culture, and experienced little social and geographical mobility. The Huguenots, through conformity to the established church and access to commercial wealth, combined a fierce pride in their own traditions with a relatively easy penetration of the host culture. Some, like the Methodists and the Quakers, owed their origins to outside influences, but soon generated their own energy and created their own indigenous communities. Thus, minorities based on religious adherence appear to have a greater ability to adapt and survive than those based on ethnicity alone.

Thirdly, it must be said that many of these post-Reformation religious minorities carried with them a strong antipathy to Roman Catholicism and state enforced religion. The fact that some of them were deliberately used to bolster the Protestant Ascendancy further isolated them from Irish Catholics. Not surprisingly, many Huguenots and Palatines were susceptible to Wesley's evangelicalism, which itself had its origins amongst those displaced Protestant minorities of Central Europe. In the nineteenth century it was not unusual to find such people at the forefront of resistance to Catholic Emancipation and other attempts to dismantle the Ascendancy. Folk memories of old persecutions and injustices linger long in migrant communities.

Finally, it is impossible to quantify the precise impact of such minorities on the wider Irish culture. But the remains of Huguenot Portarlington, Moravian Gracehill, Quaker Bessbrook, Palatine Courtmatrix and Methodist communities in south-west Ulster testify, physically at least, to the existence of living religious traditions with connections all around the globe. Irish Protestantism

The Faith Mission near Strabane,
1910. Occasional evangelical
revivals are characteristic of Irish
Protestantism.
Left: The Palatine's Cottage Door.
These humble German farmers
were given land under decidedly
favourable terms, much to the
chagrin of their native Irish
neighbours.

often bears the appearance of a parochial monolith, but it has, in fact, engagingly diverse and internationalist elements within it. Of course these minorities at their worst could be carpingly narrow and separatist, but at their best they testify to human endurance and to the power of religious motivation over unfavourable circumstances. Perhaps the sadness is not that such minorities came to Ireland but that they did not come in larger numbers and under different circumstances. Greater religious pluralism, with fewer established interests to protect, might well have made Irishmen more tolerant of one another. But then that is to wish away history, something that the Irish are never at liberty to do.

10

Twentieth-century Settlers

Jewish, Italian and Indian communities are just three of the ethnic minorities who provide the spices in today's Irish population stew: although domestic dissatisfaction may have been their original motivation, they have made a rich contribution to Irish life.

John Darby

IMAGINE the population of Ireland as a shore line. Its contours have been shaped by succeeding waves of invaders and immigrants. Celts, Normans, English, Scots – all have diverted the flow to a greater or lesser degree, and each has affected the shape of the shoreline. Again, to a greater or lesser degree, the waters carried by these waves have mingled with each other. The mixture has produced an uneasy blend of inspiration and desolation.

There is a sub-plot to this theme. Not all of Ireland's immigrants were numerous. Not all were prepared to assimilate with the society they found when they arrived. Some had cultures and practices which remained distinctive. Just as the Irish were attracted to emigration by domestic poverty and foreign opportunity, other groups were similarly attracted to Ireland.

The motivation for most emigrants sprang from domestic dissatisfaction rather than a positive attraction to Ireland. The peak of Jewish immigration followed anti-semitic pogroms in eastern Europe at the end of the nineteenth century. More recent arrivals, like Indians and Chinese during the post-war years, were attracted by Europe's relative prosperity, and Ireland got its share. Chinese are currently the most numerous immigrants, and there are small colonies of Vietnamese on both sides of the border. And so it continues. The Vietnamese war produced its refugees, and people from Sri Lanka are currently fleeing from the violence there.

A traditional dragon celebrates the beginning of the Chinese New Year on the streets of Belfast.

This chapter will deal with three groups who have, despite small numbers, made particular impact on Irish cultural and leisure activities. They are Ireland's Jewish, Italian and Indian communities.

There is no shortage of theories about when the first Jews arrived in Ireland. The most fanciful of these had Jeremiah founding Tara and depositing the Arc of the Covenant in the great mound there; hence the name of Tara was taken to be a corruption of the Jewish Torah, or Law. The historical record shows Jews in Ireland since the Middle Ages. The pattern of settlement was an uneven one: short bursts of immigration, lasting for perhaps two generations, followed by decline. In 1745, for example, around 200 Jews lived in Dublin. By 1818, according to one estimate, only two practising Jewish families remained in the city, a grocer's and a pencilmaker's. They performed their religious rites in their own houses. According to a *History of Dublin* published in 1818, 'Several efforts have been made to convert them, without success. They are honest harmless people.' If such estimates were accurate it is difficult to understand how the members of the Auxiliary Society for the Conversion of Jews, which had branches in Dublin, Sligo and Belfast in 1818, passed their time. The origins of the present community are clear enough. Most arrived from the Baltic states and eastern Europe at the turn of the last century. In the present century the number of Jews in Ireland probably never exceeded 6,000 or fell below 3,000. The current population is closer to the lower of these numbers.

It has always been predominantly an urban community, and often concentrated within towns. By 1980 Dublin's 2,000 Jews almost all lived on the south side of the Liffey. A survey of 130 of these Dublin families in 1980 presents a picture of a well-educated and self-consciously Jewish community, mostly born in Ireland. Perhaps its main characteristic was that it was an ageing community; only a third were under forty-five, and half were over sixty. The young were often better educated than their parents, and placed much less emphasis on their Jewishness. They were more likely to entertain non-Jews, and they cared less about living close to other Jews.

Two events in 1986 unconsciously symbolised these changes.

Within a matter of months, the United Hebrew Congregation synagogue in South Circular Road was sold, and Ireland's first Jewish museum was opened. If further symbolism is required, the renovated Dublin Mosque and modern Islamic Centre stands a few yards from the abandoned synagogue. The synagogue had opened in 1916, when the community was reaching its peak. Gerald Davis described the continental atmosphere in 'Little Jerusalem' in the 1940s like this:

> Sunday morning was shopping day in Clanbrassil Street; shabbily dressed men argued and gesticulated grandly, old ladies haggled in the shops, poking at chickens while they talked, feeling out the biggest 'schaltz' herring from a huge, redolent, salt-caked barrel, and swapping stories in half-English, half-Yiddish. Today, all this is past; only a handful of shops remain, mainly the butchers who deliver kosher meat to the suburbs and just one or two other predominatly Jewish shops.

This had all but disappeared by the 1960s.

The Irish have often taken pride in their toleration towards Jews. In 1915 the contributor of three long articles on the Jews in Ireland concluded with complacency:

> Our record on the Jews, some insignificant aberrations excepted, is a singularly clean one. We left them whatever molars they were possessed of. We never either blinded them completely or tore out one of their eyeballs. We never burned them – in batches or by units. We never massacred them – singly or in droves. This is a matter on which we can look the Saxon stiffly in his countenance.

Jewish memories were sometimes less benign, and indeed there is evidence of local resentment. In the early years of this century the young Gentiles from Lombard Streeet chanted the following taunt at the Jewish kids from Oakfield Place:

> 'Two shillies, two shillies,' the Jewman did cry,
> 'For a fine pair of blankets from me you did buy;
> Do you think me von idjit or von bloomin' fool,
> If I don't get my shillie I must have my vool.'

More recently, in the 1940s, A.J. Leventhal described how Jews in Dublin were 'regarded as strangers who, as such, ought to be liquidated'.

The most notable example of Irish anti-semitism, however, took place in Limerick, not Dublin. A community of Jewish refugees, mainly from Lithuania, had settled there around Coloney Street, building a synagogue in 1889. Five years later a Redemptorist priest in the town, Fr John Creagh, preached two sermons against them. In these sermons the Jewish people were charged with blasphemy, robbery, deicide and 'ritual child murder'. The sermons were followed by anti-Jewish riots in the town, during which Jews were beaten, stoned and boycotted. One hundred and thirty Jews left Limerick, and the community effectively ceased to exist.

The Cork community may have been spared such traumatic experiences, but its decline was even more dramatic. In the lifetime of Gerald Goldberg, the ex-Lord Mayor of Cork, emigration and intermarriage had reduced the community from around 500 to fourteen.

The other major Jewish community was in Belfast. Its founder was a wealthy Hamburg linen merchant, Daniel Joseph Jaffe, who built the first synagogue in 1864 in Great Victoria Street. But the people who worshipped there were mainly refugees from Russian persecution in Lithuania. His son Otto was twice elected Lord Mayor of Belfast, in 1899 and 1904. Ironically, Sir Otto Jaffe was forced to leave Belfast not because of anti-semitism but as a result of anti-German feeling during the First World War.

The size and prosperity of the Belfast community grew steadily during the twentieth century, and both the community and its synagogues moved to the city's suburbs. But the pattern of population growth has not continued. In 1960 there were just under 1,500 on the communal register of the Belfast Jewish community. In 1986 the number was closer to 200. The violence in Northern Ireland has certainly accelerated this emigration, but its root cause lies elsewhere. This is the cycle of migration of the first three generations of immigrants. The Jaffes were quite untypical of Belfast's first Jewish families. Most of them were poor and uneducated refugees from eastern Europe. But sixty years later the profile had changed. Most of the children and grand-children of the immigrants were well-educated merchants or professional people. Many moved away to Britain or the United States for reasons similar to those which attracted the Irish to the same destinations. Some moved to Israel. The effects of this emigration were drastic. In a very short time Belfast Jews were struggling to

The President of Israel, Chaim Herzog, was born in Belfast and raised in Dublin, the son of an Irish rabbi.

survive as a self-contained community. Numbers attending the Hebrew school dropped. In 1977 the Jewish Institute, which had been opened in Ashfield Gardens fifty years earlier, was burned down by vandals. Most important, the pool of Jewish marriage partners became too small and young people either sought Jewish spouses elsewhere or 'married out'. By the 1970s as many as one in three Jews were marrying outside the community.

Whatever the future holds for Irish Jews, there is no denying that they have made their marks on the past. There have been Jewish Lord Mayors in Dublin, Belfast and Cork. Chaim Herzog, President of Israel, was born in Belfast. In the Irish Republic, perhaps the most satisfying evidence of Jewish acceptance and Jewish involvement was the election of three Jewish T.D.s to the Dail in 1981. It seems almost artificially contrived and even-handed for each of the three to represent a different party. But they did: Ben Briscoe of Fianna Fail, Mervyn Taylor of Labour and Alan Shatter of Fine Gael.

The first Italian immigrants to Ireland showed no such interest in politics. Most who arrived before the middle of the last century came to provide specialist services – churchmen, bankers', terrazzo and mosaic workers. The first ice cream, for example, was brought to Ireland by Venetians and Neapolitans during the 1870s. Some Italians, like Bianconi with his network of over 100 passenger coaches, made a significant mark on Irish life. But the Italian community in Ireland dates from the 1880s, when they came in numbers from the Mezzagiorno and settled in Dublin and Belfast.

One of this group was Guiseppe Cervi, who opened a small *pensione*, or lodging house, in Little Ship Street. It was one of the few places in the city serving Italian food, so the pensione became a focus for Italians in Dublin. Around 1886 Signor Cervi opened the first chip shop in Ireland, and added an Irish clientele to his Italian one. As demand grew, family and neighbours from Italy came to join the business. By 1914 there were about fifty Italians in Dublin, enough to merit naming the area around Ship Street 'Little Italy'.

Almost all came from the small impoverished province of Frosinone, in the region of Lazio, near Rome; and a remarkably

Italians in Ireland maintained close social and political links with their homeland. This photograph shows supporters of Mussolini at a dinner in Belfast's Grand Central Hotel in 1932.
Opposite: Not all Italian immigrants sold ice-cream. This one-man-band was photographed in Kilkee, Co. Clare, around 1900.

high proportion from the area around the small village of Casalattico. Is there any part of Ireland where their family names do not produce instant salivation – Forte, Cafolla, Morelli, Divito, Fusco, Mollucca? These are Casalattico names. It is as if emigrants from Co. Leitrim were managing all the major cafés in Paris.

Different waves, especially after each of the great wars, raised the number of Italians to well over 2,500 by 1986, its peak. A survey by *Italia Stampa*, the community's magazine, confirmed that 80 per cent still had their origins in Lazio, and that around 80 per cent were in the restaurant business. Ice cream and chips required little initial capital, and members of the family provided the work force. The business suited people who, according to one, 'were too proud to work for others'.

Dublin and Belfast eventually became over-crowded with chip shops, so members of the Italian community opened up restaurants in provincial towns. By 1986, although 63 per cent still lived in Dublin, only two counties, Leitrim and Monaghan, claimed no Italians. By a process of colonisation, or evangelism, the gospel of good cheap food for working people became Italy's major contribution to Irish society.

The 1986 survey claimed that 100 Italians lived in Northern Ireland, a considerable underestimate. Nevertheless, the northern community has declined since 1970, partly because of the violence. Italians from across the border are now more likely to meet each other in Italy, where many take their holidays, than in Ireland. The desire to return to Frosinone is still strong, and a large proportion still hold Italian passports.

The sense of community persists. It is maintained by frequent visits to Italy. Unlike the Jewish immigrants, Italians often preferred their children to leave school at the earliest opportunity to work in the shop. After the second generation, however, children often became less willing to be shackled to the traditional business. In addition, there are signs that the Irish market for fish and chips is saturated. The Chinese and Indians, who provide the same hard work and cheap, slighly exotic food as the early Italian immigrants, have taken over the running.

According to folklore in the community the first Indian to settle in Ireland – a Mr Chada – arrived as recently as 1929. By 1957 his son was employing twenty-five people in the family footwear and drapery business in Derry, which had a community of about fifty Indians at that time, the largest in Ireland. Today about 600 Indians are living in the Irish Republic and just under 1,000 in Northern Ireland. This is almost exactly the number recorded twenty years earlier. Since 1970 there have been few new arrivals. The cycle of migration had virtually been completed within one generation.

The vast majority of these immigrants come from the Punjab in northern India, and as many as 75 per cent from the region of Doaba, especially the town of Hadiabad. Consequently many are related to each other. Apart from a transient population of students and doctors, most began as drapers. They sold goods on the never-never as travelling salesmen. As a community they have graduated through suitcase, stall and store. Now many own their own shops. The move into the catering trade is very recent. In 1980 Belfast had not a single Indian restaurant. By 1986 seven had opened in Belfast and eight in Dublin.

It is not easy to preserve cultural practices among such a small and dispersed community, but there has always been a determination to do so, through religious feasts and film shows. The opening of the Indian Centre in Belfast's Clifden Street in 1980 provided a focus for Indian culture – language, religion, cookery, films and other entertainment. It contains the only Hindu temple in Ireland. Nevertheless all its activities are open to the Irish community and they are well attended. The organisers of the centre are at pains to emphasise that it 'had been set up to help the Indian community mix with their Northern Ireland neighbours and to foster better relations between the two communities'.

This laudable and apparently simple objective involves a considerable skill at tightrope walking in Northern Ireland. It is not so easy to remain neutral in a society which is obsessed with allegiences and group loyalty. Indeed three members of the Indian community have been killed during the Troubles. Consequently they avoid local politics, and controversies about school selection: 'We send our children to the nearest school, or to the best school, regardless of religion.'

So the Indian community in Northern Ireland, while open to the broader society, still retains an element of self-sufficiency and non-involvement. Marriages between Indians and Irish may be increasing, but are still unusual. Family contacts are still the basis of most business operations. The balance between insularity and assimilation is being maintained.

These three communities – the Jews, Italians and Indians – with minor qualifications, came from poor countries to a relatively prosperous society. They lacked capital and specialist skills. They all took pride in their willingness to work long hours. Self-employed, they were unwilling to work for others. The consequent reliance on the family made them look homeward as their businesses prospered. Rather like a beach-head in reverse, the immigrants to Ireland came from remarkably localised homelands – Cassalattico in Italy, the area around Achmehan in Lithuania, and Doaba in India. Incidently, most of the Chinese community in Ireland came from Hong Kong's rural villages; appropriately they are known to the Cantonese as the Hakka, or strangers. This shared parochial background provided both strength and weakness. It supplied the comfort of a shared familiar religion, culture and language in a strange environment. It also provided an economic base.

Academic literature on the role of such 'middleman minorities' in other societies stresses their tendency to assume middle-rank economic roles. This was also true in Ireland. Rather than compete with the Irish for jobs, they found gaps in the economic market or created new markets: the Italians and Indians in catering; the Jews and Indians in selling clothes.

Their reactions to the Troubles in Northern Ireland are instructive. All the immigrant communities tried hard to avoid involvement in partisan politics, and their existence on the periphery of society usually made this possible. As the violence continued, some members of the older and prosperous Italian and Jewish communities decided to leave. But their places were quickly filled by new immigrants. The number of Indians was not affected, and Chinese and Vietnamese immigrants greatly increased. It is perhaps a reminder that the term 'Troubles' is a relative one.

The quality of the relationship between the ethnic minorities and the Irish host community depended on two main factors: the degree of cultural difference between the newcomers and their hosts; and the willingness of the newcomers to integrate or remain separate. The inability to speak English, at least in a manner comprehensible to the Irish, immediately marked them apart from their hosts. It also increased reliance on their fellow immigrants. So did their social and recreational habits. A love for Indian films and music was the concrete which united a geographically dispersed Indian community; Signor Cervi's Italian pasta was the lure for Dublin's early Italian immigrants. So they sometimes gravitated towards the same areas, in Dublin for example. The resulting mystique and separateness sometimes encouraged suspicion from the local population. Religion too imposed dietary and other restrictions on Jews, although Hindus were more relaxed in adapting them to this alien culture. Nevertheless none of these practices necessarily drove a barrier between immigrants and natives. That depended more on their willingness to assimilate. Consider the Indian and Jewish communities in Northern Ireland. By the 1980s their numbers were similar, and both had constructed religious and cultural centres in Belfast. The Indians regarded their centre as a potential bridge with the broader community. All its activities, including the religious ones, were open to anyone who wished to come. In the literal sense community relations were consciously on the agenda. The Jewish centre, however, was designed predominantly as a place for the Jewish community. Occasionally it was hired out to outsiders, but it was unashamedly designed for Jewish education, social intercourse and worship. Neither the community relations function nor the community preservation role is inherently superior. They are simply different, and had different consequences.

By way of contrast, members of the Jewish communities have become actively involved in party politics on both sides of the border – rather more so in the Irish Republic. The Italians and Indians, despite their general willingness to integrate, have shied clear of party involvement. They particularly emphasise their political neutrality, perhaps understandably, in Northern Ireland. The crunch point in determining the level of assimilation is the question of marriage. This is a less serious problem for the Indians and Italians, for different reasons, than for the Jews. The Indian practice of arranged marriages, with partners from India or the Indian community in Ireland, is still the most common mode, but marriages with Irish people are tolerated. Italians, especially in Dublin, often marry members of the Irish-Italian community.

Nevertheless the Italians were Catholic; and in Ireland this greatly increased the number of potential marriage partners. In Northern Ireland, where fewer Italians live, most have taken Irish partners. They continue as full members of the group. There is no stigma attached to marrying out of the community for either Indians or Italians. The Jewish boy who takes an Irish wife, however, cuts himself off from the community. Neither his wife nor his children are recognised as Jews. He himself is likely to suffer social ostracism. This strict adherence to religious precepts has had a disastrous effect. People were forced to look for partners outside Ireland, and often stayed away. Add to that the tendency for second and third generation Jews to leave for Israel or the United States, and the problem increases arithmetically. The more the community attempted to maintain itself by enforcing the very rules which defined it as a community, the more it lost members through emigration or marrying out.

There is an allied factor. In the post-war years well over three-quarters of both Indian and Italian communities in Ireland were self-employed, usually in family businesses. Some younger Italians complain about their parents removing them from school at the first opportunity to work in the shop. Some older ones admit that their strong desire to keep the family together may have played a part in this. The Jewish community, on the other hand, had moved from family businesses into the professions in three generations. And professionals are much more mobile. The contrast in attitudes towards entering the professions is striking. 'My son the doctor' is the proudest Jewish boast; but 'Gain a doctor, lose a son' is how one Italian put it.

There is a critical mass which determines the options open to minority communities. Above a certain size it is possible to support a super-structure of separate schools, shops and places of worship. But if the population falls below that size it canot sustain itself. The collapse, once started, is difficult to arrest – a sort of 'community blight' where the process of decline accelerates the decline itself. People leave before the worst happens, thereby hastening the worst. At this stage the community must compromise or collapse. It is an exaggeration to say that the Italian community has compromised, and that the Jewish communities outside Dublin have collapsed. But it is not a great exaggeration.

Such is perhaps the natural and unavoidable fate of any small

The Indian community has always been determined to preserve its culture.
This traditional Hindu wedding was celebrated in Belfast in 1987.

minority in any country. Whether they have compromised or dwindled they have enriched, and still enrich, Irish life. There are an estimated 124 ethnic restaurants in the Irish Republic alone, employing 1,329 people. The trail blazed by the Italians is currently being extended by the Chinese, and their concentration around Dame Street in Dublin suggests the imminent emergence of a 'Little Hong Kong'. The revival of street markets in Ireland over the last twenty years was sparked by immigrants from the Indian sub-continent. The contribution of the Jewish community to politics, and especially to the arts, is remarkable in view of its size.

The earlier and greater waves of immigrants – the Celts, the English, the Scots – may be the main ingredients for today's Irish population stew. The smaller communities provide the spices.

11

The People of Ireland

As in the past, the people of Ireland will continue to interact with one another and with the outside world, emigrating, receiving immigrants and settlers, quarrelling, forgetting old ways and learning new ones.

Liam de Paor

IRELAND is a European island. It shares in the long history of wars and migrations which characterises the western world. Nameless prehistoric peoples, then Celts, then Vikings, then Normans, then English, then Scots: the mixture suggests that Ireland is just like other western countries.

But it is not, quite. In spite of the admixture, the country is unusually homogeneous in the makeup of its population. It displays in this respect some of the characteristics we associate with islands. Just as Ireland is relatively poor in species of plants and animals — because the sea was a barrier to their spread — so it offers a comparatively limited range of human types, whether we are concerned with physical characteristics such as skin colour, or with mental and temperamental manifestations.

Stand at the gate of a public grade school in Pittsburgh or Toronto, or board an underground railway car in London or Paris. You are presented with a rainbow of skin colours as well as a Babel of cultural backgrounds. Now stand at equivalent school gates or board a bus in Belfast or Cork. The contrast is striking. There is a fairly uniform pinkness of face as well as a limited experience of one narrow world. We are dealing with different kinds of societies. And there is a harsher contrast, reflected in social attitudes, a contrast between an openness to variety, in those countries where great variation exists, and an intolerance of it, where variation is minimal, as in Ireland.

This is, of course, a generalisation. There exist great racial and cultural tensions in Great Britain, in France and in North America. But by and large the populations and the institutions of those countries are committed to a liberal and pluralistic view of multi-ethnic society, not perhaps because of idealism or ideology but because facts force it on them. The difference is that in Ireland the mixture is a west European mixture. The Irish are, in this respect, a fine example of cultural time-lag. The vast melting pot of peoples created in recent centuries by European empires and by the consequent great migrations of non-Europeans has not yet greatly affected them. I should like to return to this question of homogeneity; but first to address that sequence of additions to Irish human stock which has been examined stage by stage in the preceding chapters.

In discussing such a topic as 'the people of Ireland' it is difficult to strike a reasonable balance. We are reminded of this when we recollect, for example, that Peter Woodman, at the beginning of this book, in talking about 'early settlers', had to cover a period four times as long as that covered by all the other contributors combined – something like 8,000 years – to bring us only about as far as the time of Christ.

This chronological imbalance – which is the inevitable consequence both of the insufficiency and of the bias of our knowledge – should give us pause. Admittedly, prehistoric populations, apart from living a long, long time ago (and our prejudice is to diminish their importance according to their distance from us), were much smaller than modern populations. In very early prehistoric times we must be dealing with quite tiny groups. But these undoubtedly increased and multiplied, not only by increments from outside the country but by the ordinary processes of reproduction. Women bore children and, in the course of time, learned to make gardens, cultivated them to produce food, and so made possible considerable increases in population. More and more mouths could be fed, and presumably therefore there was a decline in abortion and infanticide. Peter Woodman has shown scholarly caution in his guesses at the magnitude of early populations. 'Could our populations by 2500 BC,' he asks, 'have reached 50 to 100,000?' I believe they could, and that perhaps we could even double that higher figure. But in any case, we can readily work out that in the last 8,000 years before the beginning of the

Christian era, the total number of people who lived and died in Ireland over those eighty centuries must be of the order of millions.

Peter Woodman points out that the gene pool of the Irish was probably set by the end of the Stone Age. It may well have been set quite early within the Stone Age – perhaps by about 5,000 years ago. And that gene pool is probably very closely related to the gene pools of highland Britain – of western Scotland, northern England, Wales and Cornwall. This is a survival area. It corresponds roughly to what came to be known, in the last century, as the 'Celtic fringe' – just because it was the area where Celtic languages, once widespread in Europe, lingered on into the modern period. But within that fringe area, relationships, both cultural and genetic, almost certainly go back to a much more distant time than that uncertain period when Celtic languages and customs came to dominate both Great Britain and Ireland. Therefore, so far as the physical make-up of the Irish goes, I think we may take Peter Woodman's point: that all of them, north, south, east and west in Ireland must reckon as their most significant group of ancestors those people who lived in the country before St Patrick arrived. And they share these origins with their fellows in the neighbouring parts – the north and west – of the next-door island of Great Britain.

There is much evidence to suggest that many prejudices, attitudes, superstitions and folk-customs came down from those remote ages. No doubt the prehistoric Irish had their own religious beliefs and cults, but the modern Irish might envy their distant ancestors one blessed dispensation – nobody of all those millions before the year dot could read the Bible; there was not a single Catholic or Protestant in all of Ireland.

The Celts are at once a reality and a fiction. Certainly, a significant change came about in Ireland, probably in the last millennium BC. A single language came to be spoken all over the island, related to the languages spoken at that time in Britain and on the Continent, but deriving its own distinctive individuality presumably from elements it absorbed from the older indigenous languages it replaced. The language, Irish, was used, insofar as it comes down to us in records, to give expression to the beliefs and self-aggrandising stories of a rural ruling class. We can discern immediately that these beliefs and stories are very close to those

Aspects of Irish identity shift with time. Organisers of the Ulster Unionist
Convention of 1892 apparently found no offence in a banner in Gaelic
proclaiming 'Ireland Forever', while the authorities of the Catholic seminary,
St Patrick's College, Maynooth, seemed to have no qualms about entertaining
King Edward VII and Queen Alexandra in 1903.

of the equivalent ruling classes of the time among the Britons and the Gauls. Tomás Ó Fiaich in his chapter has given an account of this factual side of the Celts.

But was there a displacement of population, with tall, blond, blue-eyed Celts coming to take over from the small dark people (if such they were) of Mesolithic and Neolithic origin? Not at all. The Celts were, at best, the Ascendancy of their day, a minority powerful enough to impose their language. They have, however, an enormous cultural importance for the history of the inhabitants of Ireland. In the first place, the language itself flourished for something like two thousand years. By the Middle Ages it was the most widely distributed language in the British Isles, being spoken throughout Ireland, throughout Scotland, and on the Isle of Man. All over that area it survives in innumerable place-names. It produced an extensive and important literature and must have been a major influence on the formation of the world-view of the peoples of Ireland and of highland Britain. Irish, in its various forms, has dwindled away over the past five hundred years until now Manx is dead and there are less than 50,000 native speakers of Gaelic in Scotland and less than half that number in Ireland. But that decline is very recent. We have moved away from the Gaelic world but it is still visible, as it were, behind us in the middle distance.

Gearoid Ó Tuathaigh has dealt very ably with some of the ways in which the Gaelic heritage has been accepted, manipulated, mythologised, denied, politicised and parodied in the comparatively recent past. Above all it was exploited to restore an ancient unity which would overcome or subsume the distinctions and divisions of modern times. Those divisions are most notoriously manifest in terms of religious confession. A sharp and cruel distinction was made, by law, in Ireland at the beginning of the eighteenth century, which set the pattern for subsequent Irish history. It was a distinction between the included Protestants and the excluded Catholics. Dissenters were excluded too and developed for a time ambiguous attitudes to the dispensation under which they found themselves.

But it was chiefly the Catholics who identified with the rapidly disintegrating Gaelic world – perhaps largely just because it was being destroyed by the new polity which excluded them. Their effort was in tune with what was happening in other parts of

Europe. All the western countries had traced their high culture from that of ancient Greece and Rome, but in the early modern period the formation of nation-states and of national ideologies led to an interest in and some glorification of the barbarian past and its peoples, including Celts, Goths, Franks and others. In England, for example, the publication in 1586 of Camden's *Brittania* marks the beginning not only of research into the unrecorded or poorly recorded past of the predecessors of the English people but also of the romantic recreation of a lost world. The very word *Brittania* – 'Britain' – is rescued from antiquity as a sign for a totality which had been broken up by the changes of time and the movements of peoples. With the union of the Scottish and English crowns in 1603 and the union of the two kingdoms in 1707, the concept of 'Britain' rapidly gained strength – romantic antiquarianism in the service of state policy to produce a new super-nationalism that would embrace England, Scotland and Wales. MacPherson's *Ossian*, which directed attention to the Gaelic Celts, was a spin-off of this process.

The complex development that Gearoid Ó Tuathaigh has traced is all the more interesting because in due course it took an unexpected direction and led not to the strengthening but to the break-up of the new nation-state that had been brought into being under the crown to encompass, after 1800, Ireland as well as England, Scotland and Wales. We can see a very recent example of a similar process in the attempts, conducted largely by Ian Adamson, to give an historical identity to the people on both sides of the North Channel through the rediscovery, or re-creation, of an ancient 'Cruthnean' nation. And we can see, comparing what Tomás Ó Fiaich has told us with what Gearoid Ó Tuathaigh has unravelled, that for modern Ireland Celtic fiction has been considerably more significant than Celtic fact, important though the fact was and is.

In moving on to 'the first influx of new peoples into Ireland since the major settlement of the Celts', as Marie-Therese Flanagan put it, we should take note first, as she does, that Ireland experienced neither Roman nor Germanic settlement. The fact that the country came down from later prehistory into the Middle Ages with a social system which was modified only by the acceptance of Christianity was to be of great and continuing importance; newcomers to Ireland right down to quite recent times were to find the land a very strange one in some ways, compared to neighbouring countries.

However in many other ways its development was parallel to and comparable with that of other parts of Europe. There was, for example, a normal centralising tendency, as a large number of small chiefdoms was brought under a few hegemonies which in turn tended toward the creation of a national state. This was re-inforced by the strong consciousness which had been developed of the island itself as a single cultural and almost mystical entity. Nation-building could proceed within boundaries which were already given, by nature and by a long-established tradition. The Gaelic world might extend into Britain, but Ireland was bounded by the sea. This powerful concept was transmitted, in the seventeenth century, by the mortally wounded Gaelic culture to the dispossessed Irish of the early modern underworld, to contribute mightily to the ideology of recent nationalism.

The Vikings almost certainly settled in smaller numbers in Ireland than in Britain; but variations in the percentages of different blood-groups in the population suggest that they may have made some impact in genetic terms, when they established trading towns round the east and south coasts in the tenth century. They certainly made an impact on the Irish polity, not by conquest, in which they were unsuccessful, but by greatly assisting a re-orientation of Ireland, particularly south-eastern Ireland, towards the outside world. Trade and traffic increased considerably in the Viking period, and with them there came not only many people from outside, but also new ideas and stirrings of change. The old inland centres, and the conservative strongholds of the monastic cities, begin to fade in relative importance. Dublin becomes what it was to remain down to the present – the chief centre of communication between Ireland and the world at large.

In a sense, the Norman take-over, studied by Lewis Warren, is just a continuation of this process. The more energetic and progressive Irish kings, competing to create a national state, were dabbling in politics and affairs outside as well as inside Ireland. And they invited and introduced the outside world. This led very quickly not only to new settlement which in some parts of the island was quite extensive, but also to what is described in current jargon as 'de-stabilisation'. The kings of England, who intervened to control the enterprises of the Norman barons, behaved in Ireland in principle much as they did in England, as Lewis Warren has pointed out. But the circumstances were wholly different, and the Irish experience contrasts sharply with the English. The

Norman conquest of 1066 and after had a unifying effect in England. The Norman incursions of 1169 and after shattered the centralisation which had just been achieved in Ireland and failed, for various reasons, to achieve a new centralisation in its place.

They accentuated contrasts which were already apparent, notably that between roughly the south-eastern half of the island and the north-western. This might very crudely be described as a contrast between that part of the island most affected by the newly implanted culture and polity and that part where the old Gaelic system remained dominant. But the contrast between a modernising south and east and an archaising north and west – between progressive and regressive – had already begun to show before the Normans arrived. This contrast was to be, if anything, strengthened in the later Middle Ages. In some ways sixteenth-century Ulster was closer to the early Iron Age than was, say, tenth-century Ulster. And, while we find a reversal at the time of the Industrial Revolution, when for a period east Ulster was the progressive part of Ireland, on the whole the pattern set in the early Middle Ages has been retained.

The Norman settlement involved some colonisation, quite intensive in some areas as the very large numbers of people whose surnames are 'Walsh' or 'Fleming' exemplify in the Waterford-Wexford-Kilkenny area. And even though much of the settlement failed, for one reason or another, in the later Middle Ages, it left a permanent mark on the landscapes it affected, and also on the institutions and outlook of Ireland. Even in those parts of the country where Gaelic law, speech, custom and tradition prevailed undisturbed, Norman social and cultural influence penetrated.

The distinction between Norman and English in medieval Ireland is by no means clearcut, all the more so since it is a distinction made more by modern writers and commentators than by those of the Middle Ages. Aidan Clarke, in discussing the complex question of the English in Ireland, introduces his chapter aptly with a quotation from Maurice Fitzgerald in 1170: 'Just as we are English to the Irish, so we are Irish to the English.' In medieval Ireland the English who settled, in and out of the towns, were consciously a colony, and, in medieval terms, a distinct 'nation' in Ireland. However, they were a part of Ireland, and there was a recurring problem which arose from their frequent resentment at the attitudes, behaviour and bungling of the English of England –

people who came over from England, as officials or otherwise, to conduct government business in Ireland.

The peculiar problems of colonial 'kith and kin' which we have seen from time to time in the modern world can be observed in the Irish Middle Ages. There was the problem too of preserving the colonial English identity from being overwhelmed by the dominant Gaelic culture of the country. In the church the problem led to divisions which in an odd way prefigured the Catholic-Protestant division of later times. There was only one church, with one doctrine, and, in theory, one sytem of authority. But in practice there were two distinct church organisations, one for each of the two nations in medieval Ireland. Since the medieval English colony, by and large, remained Catholic at the Reformation, its subsequent history is ironic.

The Old English, as they came to be called, maintained their colonial distinction from the Gaelic Irish, or tried to. They took whole-heartedly to the new modes and manners of the Counter-Reformation, as, to such an extent, the Gaelic Irish did not, so that even after the Reformation it could still be said that – in a way – there were two different kinds of Roman Catholic church in Ireland. But even being a distinctive kind of Roman Catholic did not save the Old English, in spite of their own wishes, from being forced by the pressures of religion-linked politics into alliance with and ultimately into sharing the fate of the Gaelic Irish.

Finlay Holmes has dealt with the Scottish-Irish connection which of course assumed a special significance and importance at the time of the seventeenth-century plantations in Ulster. These, as everyone knows, have done much to shape recent Irish history. But the link between Ulster and Scotland is by no means of modern origin. It goes back as far as we can trace the human story in Ireland. The narrow channel at the head of the Irish Sea issues into an archipelago whose islands, spread over the waters that link the main Irish coast to the main Scottish coast, invite the view that this is a single ocean-founded region. Throughout history the people of these islands and coasts have moved to and fro, settling now here, now there. That clumsy hyphenation 'Scots-Irish', applied in America to the Ulster Presbyterian settlers there, has real meaning in Ireland.

Those who came from Scotland to Ulster in the seventeenth-century plantations therefore were not really introducing a new element to Ireland or to the people of Ireland, although those who came in the same plantations from England to a certain extent were. The Scots found in Ulster houses, customs and traditions very like those of the Scotland they had left. That most of the Ulster people of the time were Catholics, while the incoming Scots were Calvinists, was the most obvious and striking contrast between them, as it has remained. As the Canadian anthropologist Elliott Leyton has put it, in his study of Catholics and Protestants in a fishing village on the east coast of Ulster, the two groups, while pointing up their difference on religion and many other matters, acknowledge that they are – and this he uses as the title of his book – 'the one blood'.

J. C. Beckett has dealt with another hyphenated group, the 'Anglo-Irish'. That term is, as he points out, a bad and inadequate one, which serves however, in a somewhat vague sort of way, to describe the descendants of that group which, at the end of the eighteenth century, came to be described as 'the Protestant Ascendancy'. It is a bad term not only because it is a clumsy hyphenation but because it has concealed within it a singularly misguided nationalist prejudice which will admit to the designation 'Irish' only the people of one Irish tradition.

Words like 'Scots-Irish' and 'Anglo-Irish' show that we have encountered a difficulty. The difficulty is what has commonly been termed 'the Irish problem', and the stammering expressions show that at this stage of the exposition we have stumbled upon it.

'Anglo-Irish', then, were Irish Anglicans, mainly of the gentry or upper middle classes, who acquired their hyphen because for the most part they assumed responsibility both for the running of the affairs of Ireland – for which they felt themselves uniquely competent – and for the Union, the Empire and the furtherance of England's interests in the world. The hyphen attempts to span what came to be the horns of a dilemma; once a large majority of Irish people made it plain that they did not wish Ireland to be associated intimately with England, a choice had to be made, the hyphen broken.

The Anglo-Irish originated as the second English colony in Ireland – it was the class which succeeded the displaced Catholic proprietors (both Old English and Gaelic Irish) and their followers after the seventeenth-century confiscations. Like the first colony it was English-speaking. Unlike it, it differed from the mass of the people in religion and it was a successfully dominant minority. Its language advanced, steadily and effectively; its members held property and power; it was a wholly successful colonial elite for quite a long period.

It is not too great an exaggeration to say that the Anglo-Irish made modern Ireland. J. C. Beckett has shown how much they did in building, in culture, in literature, to bring honour to what they thought of, as much as did other groups, as their country. But, as a class, they have lost influence and have greatly diminished in numbers. They leave to the present-day Irish not so much descendants among the people of Ireland as works.

The Protestant Ascendancy was by no means all of Protestant Ireland, and David Hempton has addressed himself to the history of the religious minorities, whose influence on the scene has been considerable, although their numbers were not great. Huguenots, Methodists, Quakers and others both contributed to the lively diversity of Irish Protestantism and many of them also played a special part in the economic history of the country. They also have a very large significance as emigrants, since they tended to be comparatively mobile groups and they brought their beliefs and enthusiasms to the New World, where their numbers and influence could expand much more than at home.

Ireland today, divided as it is into two jurisdictions, is yet, as I suggested at the beginning, homogeneous in the make-up of its people when compared with many of the countries of the modern world. John Darby has examined three of the small (and recently established) groups which provide the exception to this — the Jewish, Italian and Indian communities. Perhaps in the future Ireland will become a much more varied place because of settlements like those which founded these Irish communities; but at the moment this is not happening to any great extent.

It is hardly necessary to emphasise that in spite of the kind of homogeneity I have described, Ireland is a sharply divided country. That, in fact, is commonly the first and often the last thing that people round the world know about the Irish. Is it correct at all, then, to speak of 'the people of Ireland', or should we rather refer to 'the *peoples* of Ireland'? Well, if we are looking back over the country's history, I think it makes better sense to speak of 'the peoples of Ireland', because from prehistory to modern times many population groups, distinct from one another in origin, in speech, in faith, in culture, have settled or succeeded one another in Ireland. These chapters have been arranged chronologically too, but I think their emphasis is different. They say that all these elements have gone into the making of the people who now live in Ireland and they help to explain some of the characteristics, outlooks and attitudes of the late-twentieth-century Irish.

So is there one Irish people, or are there two or more peoples on the island? Or what does this question mean? There are one or two differences, to take two politicians as examples, between Ian Paisley and Peter Barry. They give allegiance to two different sovereignties. They belong to different Christian confessions. They disagree about the Anglo-Irish Agreement. But you would not mistake either of them for an Englishman, hardly for a Scotsman or a Welshman, and certainly not for a Spaniard or a Korean. There are, in other words, certain similarities. For the various groups that came to make up the Irish population did not, on this small island, remain distinct and discrete – or not for long in any case. They intermarried and interacted in a thousand ways. Each influenced and modified the culture and behaviour of the others. Before modern technology and communications opened up the possibility for the whole world to share the same football games, pop tunes and fast foods, such interactions took place rather more slowly. But Ireland is a comparatively small island, and, even in earlier ages, what was taking place in one part of it tended in due course to have an effect throughout. Not only do the Irish share 'the one blood' but they stand on the same ground – the 'narrow ground' as A. T. Q. Stewart described it for Ulster.

This is not to deny the differences and distinctions – which have been fully brought out in this book – nor necessarily to suggest that because people have a great deal in common they should belong to the same political community. There is another kind of community – people, for example, who can handle without difficulty the pronunciation of the letter-groups 'gh' and 'ch', although they might balk at 'th'; people who can instantly grasp an irony that would baffle any good literal-minded American; people who have such an intimate understanding of a political opponent and mortal foe that they can, without thinking about it, find exactly the right insult to wound. There is a shared culture

Mrs Tonhu Thong, a member of Ireland's most recent immigrant community, the Vietnamese 'boat people', receives her certificate of Irish citizenship in Dublin in July 1987.

which is Irish, just as there is a shared culture which is global, and just as there are cultural and social items which one group may not share with its fellows in Ireland, but may share with groups in Scotland, England or elsewhere.

This is why it would be perfectly accurate, for example, for a Fermanagh Protestant to say that the fields down the road are in the territory of another state, but both inaccurate and a sad misuse of the English language for him to say that they are in a foreign country. This is why it is plain silly, as well as implying a barbarous advocacy of the virtues of ignorance, for an Ulster loyalist to refer to the Irish language as 'an archaic tribal dialect' or the like. Such extravagant statements are understandable; they are a defence against being 'got at' through an approach on the cultural flank, as it were. And such approaches are constantly, and I believe mistakenly, made. I am not, however, attempting one now.

Boundaries are necessary and convenient political devices. They serve to mark the exact limit of one jurisdiction and the beginning perhaps of another one. But even when they are supplied by nature, like the sea round Ireland, they are wholly inadequate to define the shadings of all the complexities of human societies into one another.

There is however one distinction at the moment, which is quite marked and which is reasonably well delineated by the border. The homogeneity I referred to is much stronger in the Republic than in Northern Ireland in at least one major respect. For reasons which are by no means as simple as they are sometimes made out to be, there are now comparatively few Protestants in the Republic. If I may reverse a commonly used and slightly offensive term, there is a vast and overwhelming non-Protestant majority. This has occurred in considerable part since partition; although, of course, partition was based on a large discrepancy between the proportions of Catholics and Protestants in the population of part of Ulster and the population of the rest of Ireland – with the related political differences.

But considerable demographic change has happened in Ireland, north and south, in the period since partition, and such changes continue unpredictably. I doubt if we can continue much longer to found our understanding of Ireland on the map of religious denominations. History is change, and history will not stop for us, much as some of us might like it to do so. The people of Ireland will continue to interact with one another and with the outside world, emigrating, receiving immigrants and settlers, quarrelling, forgetting old ways and learning new ones, behaving like people anywhere.

The Contributors

PETER WOODMAN is Professor of Archaeology at University College, Cork. Well known for his excavation of the mesolithic site at Mountsandel, he also wrote and introduced the recent television series *From Stone to Stone*.

TOMÁS Ó FIAICH, Archbishop of Armagh and Primate of all Ireland, is also a former Professor of History at St Patrick's College, Maynooth.

GEAROID Ó TUATHAIGH is Lecturer in Modern History at University College, Galway and author of *Ireland before the Famine 1798-1848* (1972).

MARIE THERESE FLANAGAN is Lecturer in Modern History at Queen's University, Belfast and a graduate of University College, Dublin and Oxford University.

LEWIS WARREN is Professor of Modern History at Queen's University, Belfast. The author of *Henry II* (1973) and *Norman and Angevin England, 1086-1272* (1987), he has also written and presented the BBC television series *The Normans*.

FINLAY HOLMES is Professor of Church History at the Union Theological College, Belfast and author of *Henry Cooke* (1981).

AIDAN CLARKE, Erasmus Smith's Professor of Modern History at Trinity College, Dublin, is the author of *The Old English in Ireland, 1625-42* (1966).

J. C. BECKETT is Emeritus Professor of Irish History at Queen's University, Belfast. Among his many publications are *The Making of Modern Ireland* (1966) and *The Anglo-Irish Tradition* (1976).

DAVID HEMPTON, Lecturer in Modern History at Queen's University, Belfast, is the author of *Methodism and Politics in British Society* (1987).

JOHN DARBY is Professor of Social Administration and Director of the Centre for the Study of Conflict at the University of Ulster. His publications include, as editor, *Northern Ireland: The Background to the Conflict* (1983).

LIAM DE PAOR, formerly Lecturer in History at University College, Dublin, has done much to popularise historical research in recent years. Among his publications are *Early Christian Ireland* (1958).

Further Reading

Prehistoric Settlers

Clarke, D. V., Cowie, T. G. and Foxon, A., *Symbols of Power*, Edinburgh, 1985

Eogan, G., *Knowth and the Passage Tombs of Ireland*, London, 1986

Historic Monuments of Northern Ireland, HMSO, Belfast, 1984

Mitchell, G. F., *Reading the Irish Landscape*, Dublin, 1986

O'Kelly, M. J., *Excavations at Newgrange*, London, 1982

Ó Riordáin, S. P., *Antiquities of the Irish Countryside*, New York, 1979

Raftery, B., *La Tene in Ireland*, Marburg, 1984

Woodman, P. C., *Excavations at Mount Sandel, Northern Ireland*, Belfast, 1985

The Celts

Barth, F., *Ethnic Groups and Boundaries*, London, 1969

Curtis, L. P., *Anglo-Saxons and Celts*, Connecticut, 1968

Curtis, L. P., *Apes and Angels: The Irishman in Victorian Caricature*, London, 1971

Deane, S., *Celtic Revivals*, London, 1985

Evans, E. Estyn, *The Personality of Ireland*, Cambridge, 1973

Leerson, J. T., *Mere Irish and Fior-Ghael*, Amsterdam, 1986

Lyons, F. S. L., *Culture and Anarchy in Ireland 1890-1939*, Oxford, 1979

MacDonagh, O., *States of Mind*, London, 1983

Ó Tuathaigh, M. A. G., (ed.), *Community, Culture and Conflict in Ireland*, Galway, 1986

Walsh, M. Kerney, *Destruction by Peace*, Dublin, 1986

The Vikings

Logan, F. D., *The Vikings in History*, London, 1983

Moody, T. W., Martin, F. X. and Byrne, F. J., (eds.), *A New History of Ireland, vol IX: Maps, genealogies, lists: a companion to Irish History part II*, Oxford, 1984 (maps 20-22)

Ó Corráin, D., *Ireland before the Normans*, Dublin, 1972

Ó Cuív, B., (ed.), *The impact of the Scandinavian invasions on the Celtic-speaking peoples c. 800-1100 AD*, Dublin, 1975

Todd, J. H., (ed.), *Cogadh Gaedhel re Gallaibh: The war of the Gaedhil with the Gaill*, London, 1867

The Normans

Allen Brown, R., *The Normans*, Woodbridge, 1984

Barrow, G. W. S., *Kingship and Unity: Scotland 1000-1306*, (The New History of Scotland 2), London, 1981

Davis, R. H. C., *The Normans and their Myth*, London, 1976

Douglas, D. C., *The Norman Achievement, 1050-1100*, London, 1969

Graeme Ritchie, R. L., *The Normans in Scotland*, Edinburgh, 1954

Frame, R., *Colonial Ireland, 1169-1369 (Helicon History of Ireland)*, Dublin, 1981

Lydon, J., *The Lordship of Ireland in the Middle Ages*, Dublin, 1972

Nicholls, K., *Gaelic and Gaelicised Ireland in the Middle Ages (Gill History of Ireland 4)*, Dublin, 1972

Watt, J., *The Church in Medieval Ireland (Gill History of Ireland 5)*, Dublin, 1972

Rowley, T., *The Norman Heritage 1055-1200*, London, 1983

The Scots

Adams, G. B., (ed.), *Ulster Dialects*, Cultra, 1964

Brooke, P., *Ulster Presbyterianism*, Dublin, 1987

Brown, T., *Northern Voices: Poets from Ulster*, Dublin and New Jersey, 1975

Green, E. R. R., (ed.), *Essays in Scotch-Irish History*, London, 1969

Holmes, R. F. G., *Our Irish Presbyterian Heritage*, Belfast, 1985

Leyburn, J. G., *The Scotch-Irish. A Social History*, Chapel Hill, 1962

Miller, D., *Queen's Rebels: Ulster Loyalism in Historical Perspective*, Dublin and New York, 1978

Perceval-Maxwell, M., *The Scottish Migrations to Ulster in the Reign of James I*, London, 1973

Robinson, P., *The Plantation of Ulster*, Dublin and New York, 1969

Stewart, A. T. Q., *The Narrow Ground: Aspects of Ulster, 1609-1969*, London, 1977

The English

Brady, C. and Gillespie, R., (eds.), *Natives and Newcomers: The Making of Irish Colonial Society, 1534-1641*, Dublin 1986

Canny, N. P., *The Formation of the Old English Elite in Ireland*, Dublin, 1975

Clarke, A., *The Old English in Ireland, 1625-42*, London, 1966

Cosgrove, A., (ed.), *A New History of Ireland, vol. II: Medieval Ireland, 1169-1534*, Oxford, 1987

Cosgrove, A., *Late Medieval Ireland, 1370-1541*, Dublin, 1981

Frame, R., *Colonial Ireland, 1169-1369*, (Helican History of Ireland), Dublin, 1981

Lydon, J. F., *The Lordship of Ireland in the Middle Ages*, Dublin, 1984

Lydon, J. F., (ed.), *The English in Medieval Ireland*, Dublin, 1984

Moody, T. W., Martin, F. X. and Byrne, F. J., (eds.), *A New History of Ireland, vol. III: Early Modern Ireland, 1534-1690*, Oxford, 1976

Nicholls, K., *Gaelic and Gaelicised Ireland in the Middle Ages*, (Gill History of Ireland 4), Dublin, 1972

The Anglo-Irish

Beckett, J. C., *The Anglo-Irish Tradition*, London, 1976 and Belfast, 1982

Craig, M., *Dublin 1660-1860*, Dublin, 1952

Falkiner, C. Litton, *Illustrations of Irish History and Topography*, London, 1904

Ferguson, O. W., *Jonathan Swift and Ireland*, Illinois, 1962

Landa, L. A., *Swift and the Church of Ireland*, Oxford, 1954

Religious Minorities

Beckett, J. C., *Protestant Dissent in Ireland 1687-1780*, London, 1948

Crookshank, C. H., *History of Methodism in Ireland*, Belfast, 1885-8

Grubb, I., *Quakers in Ireland, 1654-1900*, London, 1927

Harrison, R. S., *Irish Anti-war Movements*, Dublin, 1986

Hempton, D., *Methodism and Politics in British Society*, London, 1987

Hutton, J. E., *A History of the Moravian Church*, London, 1909

Jeffery, F., *Irish Methodism*, Belfast, 1964

Lee, G. L., *The Huguenot Settlements in Ireland*, London, 1936

Maguire, W. A. *et al.*, *The Huguenots and Ulster, 1685-1985*, Lisburn, 1986

Scouloudi, I., (ed.), *The Huguenots in Britain, 1550-1750*, London, 1986

Taggert, N. W., *The Irish in World Methodism, 1760-1900*, London, 1986

Twentieth-century Settlers

Davis, G., 'On being Jewish in Ireland', Everyman, 1968

Irish-Jewish Year Book, Herzog House, Zion Road, Dublin 6

Italia Stampa, Fir House, Mespil Flats, Dublin 4

Leventhal, A. J., 'What it means to be a Jew', *The Bell*, 10, 1945, 207-216

Salmon, J., 'Jews in Ireland', *Belfast Evening Telegraph*, September 24, 25 and 29, 1915

Turner, J. and Bonacich, E., 'Towards a Composite Theory of Middlemen Minorities', *Ethnicity*, 144-58, 1980

Warburton, Whitelaw and Walsh, *History of Dublin*, Dublin 1818

Waterman, S., 'Neighbourhood, Communities and Residential Change Decisions in the Dublin Jewish Community', *Irish Geography*, 16, 1983

Index